SR-71 BLACKBIRD

By Jim Goodall
Color By Don Greer

squadron/signal publications

A SR-71 Blackbird flies near the edge of space on a reconnaissance mission. The Blackbird was the fastest operational aircraft ever to serve with the USAF.

Acknowledgments

I want to thank my friends in the Air Force, CIA and Lockheed/ADP who helped me over the last 30 years in gathering information on the Blackbird program. Without the help of these special people, this labor of love would never have gotten off the ground.

Clarence L. "Kelly" Johnson, Lockheed Skunk Works
Ben R. Rich, Lockheed Skunk Works
Lou Schalk, Lockheed A-12 Test Pilot, first to fly the A-12 Blackbird
James Eastham, Lockheed A-12/YF-12 Test Pilot, first to fly the YF-12
Robert J. Gilliland, Lockheed SR-71 Test Pilot, first to fly the SR-7l

Buddy L. Brown	William Fox
Ken Collins	Joe Daley
Dennis B. Sullivan	Ronald J.(Jack) Layton
Mel Vojvodich	Frank Murray
Hugh C. Slater	Ray Schrecengost
Roger Anderson	Ben Bowles
David E. Fruehauf	Lanny Jenkins
Denny Lombard	Jerry Tyree
Arne Gunderson	David Lux
Mike Relja	John Andrews
Jay Miller	Tom Brewer
Marty Isham	Tony Landis
Tom Long	Dave Menard
Donald S. McGarry	Charles B. Mayer
Warren Munkasy	Dave Prettyman
Mike Quan	Brian C. "Buck" Rogers
Mick Roth	James Perry Stevenson
Bill Sweetman	Doug Slowiak
Toshiyuki Toda	Nicholas J. Waters III

Alicia and Jamey Goodall

ISBN 0-89747-338-8

If you have any photographs of aircraft, armor, soldiers or ships of any nation, particularly wartime snapshots, why not share them with us and help make Squadron/Signal's books all the more interesting and complete in the future. Any photograph sent to us will be copied and the original returned. The donor will be fully credited for any photos used. Please send them to:

Squadron/Signal Publications, Inc.
1115 Crowley Drive
Carrollton, TX 75011-5010

Dedication

To my daughter, Alicia Noel Goodall

The Author, James C. Goodall sitting in the cockpit of the eighth production A-12. Jim is the Crew Chief of A-12 number 128/06931, which is on display at the Minnesota Air Guard Museum located at the Minneapolis/St. Paul International Airport, St. Paul, MN. (Charles B. Mayer)

Introduction

In 1953, military aviation was in a transition from subsonic to supersonic flight. Chance-Vought had delivered the last propeller driven fighter; a F4U Corsair, to the Navy that February. In May, just three months later, the first YF-100A Super Saber was delivered to the U.S. Air Force. This was the start of the Century series fighters. This transition was made possible by the development of more powerful turbojet engines such as the Pratt & Whitney J-57, which went into production during 1953. You could now go higher, faster and farther than ever before possible. Higher altitudes meant less risk for the bombers and future reconnaissance aircraft. As far back as 1953, the altitude goal most frequently mentioned during that period was 30,000 meters or 97,000 feet. Greater range was not neglected as a design goal, but with inflight refueling, the need for range could be compromised in favor of other design goals.

With the outbreak of the Korean war, John D. Seaberg, an aeronautical engineer at Chance-Vought, was called to active duty as a major in the Air Force. Major Seaberg's first assignment was to Wright Field as part of a new development office for bombardment aircraft. What Seaberg saw in the new generation of turbojet engines, with their inherent high altitude potential, was the opportunity of match engine and airfoil (wing shape) to achieve an aircraft of low wing-loading which would be capable of operations at higher altitudes than anything yet conceived. The ideal application for such an aircraft was reconnaissance, where its high altitude capability would make detection very difficult and provide protection from interception until effective electronic counter measures were developed.

By March of 1953, Seaberg's idea had jelled into a set of specifications for preliminary design studies by aircraft manufacturers. Operational conditions specified in the requirement were an altitude of 70,000 feet or higher, a range of 1,750 miles and subsonic speeds. The aircraft would carry a crew of one and a photo reconnaissance bay capable of holding equipment weighing between 100 and 700 pounds. No armament or ejection seat would be used in order to keep the gross weight of the aircraft to an absolute minimum. The high operational ceiling would offer a form of protection, at least until the events of 1

Mr. Kelly Johnson, father of the Lockheed "Skunk Works" from its inception in 1943 until his retirement in 1973. He was directly responsible for such aircraft as the F-80, F-104, U-2 and SR-71 to name just a few. (Lockheed)

The original U-2 in NACA markings and carrying a NACA tail number, 320. At the time it carried these markings, the aircraft was being tested at Area 51, Groom Dry Lake Test Facility in Nevada. (Lockheed)

May 1960. The air frame contractors were to supply design specifications suitable for a development contract using the recommended engine, the Pratt & Whitney J-57-P19.

It was decided to bypass the larger air frame manufacturers in favor of smaller companies because the production runs would be small, and they felt the smaller firms would give the study a higher priority. There was no open bidding: Bell Aircraft, Fairchild Aircraft and the Glenn L. Martin Company were called in to discuss the studies. All three expressed strong interests in the project. The Air Force talked to no one else. Contracts were let to the three companies starting on 1 July 1953 and ran to the end of the calendar year. Bell and Fairchild were asked to design a totally new aircraft, while Martin, builder of the B-57 bomber and RB-57 reconnaissance variant, was asked to study modifications to the RB-57 that would meet the new requirements.

In early May of 1954, a new proposal for a high-altitude aircraft from Kelly Johnson's Lockheed "Skunk Works" had reached Seaberg's desk with a request for evaluation. As it would later turn out, a series of events in aeronautics, politics and diplomacy would all work in favor of Kelly's proposal.

Kelly's unsolicited proposal came as no surprise to the officers at Wright Field. Kelly had the confidence of and was accustomed to dealing with the highest levels in the Air Force and there was no reason for these officers to hide their interest in very high-altitude flight from him. He had designed and built the prototype of the first U.S. jet fighter, the P-80, in 143 days. He had gone on to design the F-90, the F-104 and the Connie to name just a few. Kelly had his very own special brand of management, which broke down to, "be quick, be quite and be on time."

Kelly's design would be based on his F-104 design, utilizing the same fuselage, a much larger wing (needed to achieve an altitude of 65,000 feet), and the General Electric J-73 turbojet engine. Seaberg was not impressed with Kelly's selection of the J-73 for extremely high altitude flight. He felt the more powerful Pratt & Whitney J-57, modified for high altitude operation was required. There was one problem with the request, the J-57 was too large to fit into the F-104's fuselage, so an air frame redesign would be required. With the go ahead given for the Martin RB-57 and the Bell X-l6, Seaberg saw no need for a third design, and recommended against Kelly's design. This view was supported by the Air Force. The Martin RB-57D was built in small numbers and the Bell X-16 was initiated but canceled in mid-1956.

After the Air Force turned Kelly's design down, he didn't give up and a fortunate turn of events gave him a big break. During 1954, the role of the guided missile was rising very fast and the Department of Defense formed a number of advisory groups to determine the impact that missiles would have on military planning and weapons. James R. Killjan became the chairman of a committee on surprise attack, and was aided by several panels. It was during the course of this work that the Intelligence Panel learned about Kelly's design proposal for a high altitude reconnaissance aircraft, and they liked it. It was known that the aircraft had been proposed to the Air Force but that the Air Force had decided not to develop it. Kelly's proposal was taken to President

The U.S. Government will still not admit this facility exists. This is the Groom Dry Lake Test Facility, also known as Area 51, as it looked in September of 1968. (USGS/Author's Collection)

Eisenhower during the latter part of November 1954.

Eisenhower decided that the funding and direction of the project would be under the control of the CIA and Richard M. Bissell, Jr. was selected to head the project. The Air Force was to contract with Lockheed for the development of the aircraft under the designation, U-2. On 9 December 1954, Trevor Gardner, assistant Secretary of the Air Force for research and development, paid a visit to Lockheed to meet with Robert Gross and Kelly Johnson. The purpose of the visit was to give them the go ahead on the design.

By the end of 1955, the Air Force had in progress a number of research and development activities based on the feasibility of using liquid hydrogen in flight. Kelly Johnson's "Skunk Works," located at Lockheed's Burbank facility, had passed their peak effort in designing and building the prototype U-2 for the CIA, and was two months into a three month design study for a liquid hydrogen fueled aircraft for Garrett. United Aircraft (now United Technologies) was in the second quarter of a study aimed at using hydrogen in a conventional turbojet engine.

The Air Force and NACA (now NASA) agreed that the Lewis laboratory would determine the feasibility of flying an aircraft fueled with liquid hydrogen. The Air Force would provide the estimated one million dollars needed for the study as well as the loan of whatever equipment was necessary.

The largest and most extraordinary project for using hydrogen as a fuel was carried out by the Air Force during the 1956-1958 time frame in super secrecy. Very few people are even aware of the program some thirty-five years later. It is estimated that the project cost upwards of 300 million dollars in 1956 dollars. This project was known by the code-name SUNTAN and even the name was classified. It had all the air of a cloak and dagger melodrama and indeed, its primary reason was just that. SUNTAN was an effort by the Air Force to develop a hydrogen fueled aircraft with performance superior to that of the super secret U-2 spy plane.

The driving force behind the Air Force's mounting interest in hydrogen fueled aircraft was the determination to develop an aircraft with superior performance to the U-2, since they were dissatisfied with their supporting role to the CIA in U-2 operations. The Air Force not only sought to take over U-2 operations, but to regain the initiative in reconnaissance equipment by developing a second generation high altitude reconnaissance aircraft. By late 1955, the time was ripe for a new proposal and soon one was made by Kelly Johnson.

The high flying U-2 was the latest symbol of Kelly Johnson's ability to design and build a new airplane quickly in his unique and unconventional "Skunk Works." Familiar with hydrogen from conduction aircraft design studies for companies like Garrett, Kelly was impressed with its potential. Early in 1956, armed with a proposal for a hydrogen fueled supersonic follow-on to the U-2, he visited the Pentagon where he had no problem in seeing high Air Force officials, including Lieutenant General Donald L. Putt, the deputy chief of staff for development. Kelly offered to build two prototype hydrogen-fueled aircraft with the first to fly within eighteen months. They would be capable of flight at 98,600 feet with a design cruising speed of Mach 2.5 and a range of 2,500 miles. To the Air Force, which had missed the opportunity to buy the original U-2, the offer was too tempting to resist, they bought it. The need for Mach 3 flight was born and Kelly went to work on the CL 400.

OXCART, CYGNUS, ROAD-RUNNER -- The A-12

OXCART requirements: launch from the desert southwest, refuel over the pole, fly to the Black Sea, return to the pole to refuel and recover back at a location in the Nevada desert.

Once upon a time, there was this CIA photographer named Gordon Mathies. His job was to float across Russia in a balloon. The balloons were of an all plastic construction, manned by either one or two recon specialists and they were launched at night. Their clandestine purpose, to over fly the Soviet Union.

The early designs suffered from pitch up problems and one of the proposed fixes was the use canards as shown on this early wind tunnel model. The air intakes were so sensitive to airflow disruptions that this configuration was never really given much serious consideration. (Lockheed via Tony Landis)

This was the final configuration of the A-12, which differed only slightly from the production aircraft. The major changes were the inner wing to fuselage blend, a full moving tail verse tail rudders, the droop on the outer wing assembly that added to low speed stability and the overall size of the elevon on the trailing edge of the inter and outer wing panels. (Lockheed via Tony Landis)

In retrospect, this turned out to be the first real "Stealth" recon aircraft of its day. No noise, non-metallic construction, high altitude and, best of all, low cost.

The birth of the first of the incredible Blackbirds began as early as the first U-2 flights. The U-2's designers knew that in order to have free access over the skies of the USSR they, and the CIA, had to improve on the drawbacks of the current U-2 design.

It was apparent even back then that the surest way to overcome the shortcomings of the U-2 was to design a totally new manned platform that could be custom tuned to the particular profile of each mission, and remain immune to the ever increasing Soviet anti-aircraft fire and surface-to-air (SAM) missiles.

From studies made to identify the type of aircraft needed, the CIA, in conjunction with Lockheed, identified and put forth the basic requirements for what became the A-12. Cruising speed: Mach 3 to Mach 4, cruise altitude: 80,000 to 100,000 feet. To meet this requirement, they employed the very latest technology money could buy. The aircraft would have a minimal radar cross section, state of the art countermeasures, new and advanced cameras and other sensors, with the ability to communicate and navigate where man had never flown before.

Lockheed and Convair were asked to submit definite proposals, funds were made available to them and the project took on the code-name GUSTO.

If Hertz had only known what their rental cars went through. This is the twenty-fourth test of the Lockreed developed SR-1 ejection seat being tested at the Groom Lake Test Facility at Area 51. The 1961 Thunderbird was courtesy of Hertz. (Author's Collection)

The A-12 rear fuselage manufacturing area of the Lockheed "Skunk Works" production area located in building 309/310 at the Hollywood Burbank Airport during 1961. (Author's Collection)

The specific date of the birth of the A-12 was sometime in the Fall of 1957. Both Lockheed and General Dynamics were asked to respond to a general operational requirement for a high speed, high-altitude reconnaissance aircraft. General Dynamics Corporation had on the drawing boards and in the wind tunnels of Fort Worth designs that, if given the chance to fly, would go higher and faster, and in some cases much faster then any of the Lockheed designs.

By mid 1959, Kelly Johnson had the ball in his court. He assembled a team of specialists, all hand picked, to take this titanium airplane from the drawing board to the air in record time. On 29 August 1959, Lockheed was declared the winner and given the go-ahead to build the first six A-12 aircraft.

A-12 number 131/06937 undergoes final assembly and systems checks at the Lockheed "Skunk Works" on 29 April 1963. (Author's Collection)

This area included both the A-12 and YF-12A manufacturing lines. The YF-12A (left) is the second YF-12A number 1002/06935 and the A-12 is number 133/06939 the last A-12 to be built. The fixture in the foreground is the main fuselage transporter trailer cover, which was used in moving all the Blackbirds to either Area 51 at Groom Lake for the A-12s and YF-12As or to the SR-71 Flight Test Facility at Air Force Plant 41, Site 2, Palmdale, California for the SR-71s. (Author's Collection)

Once the basic design had been established and finalized, all the extra equipment had to go on and in it. Each specialist was given his own area of responsibility. The cockpit started out as an empty box with the man responsible for its layout given all the necessary instruments in paper cutout form. His basic instructions were to put them where he felt they should be. The A-12's cockpit was laid out using standard dial type instruments with digital readouts for most of the functions. The digital readouts were fine if you were sitting at an altitude try to figure out your fuel consumption. If; however, you were in a crisis situation, then the standard round dials were the only way to go.

One questions has been asked time and time again. How did they build the A-12 in Burbank and get it to the middle of the Nevada desert without anyone finding out? The key to their success, was to leave Burbank on Wednesday mornings at 2:30 AM. That time turned out to be the absolute best in terms of the least amount of traffic on the LA freeway system. Once out in the desert, no one cared about the thirty-five foot wide 120 foot long tractor and box going through the desert.

After their arrival at Groom Dry Lake on 28. February 1962, it took approximately sixty days to reassemble the first aircraft; number 121. The first unofficial flight was on 25 April 1962 during a high speed taxi test. Kelly was going to have a successful first flight, no matter what.

The A-12 in the center was the last A-12, number 133/06939, while the aircraft to the left is the very first SR-71A number 2001/17950. (Author's Collection)

The aircraft in the foreground is the last A-12 to be manufactured, number 133/06939, just behind it is the M-21 "Mother" aircraft used in the TAGBOARD Program with the D-21 drone. Because of the sensitivity of the TAGBOARD mission, the final assembly area was cordoned off from the rest of the production floor much like they did with the YF-12A. (Lockheed via Tony Landis)

He definitely did not want to pull up the gear. He was still worried about a successful first flight. The A-12 was flown in a neutrally stable condition and there was some hesitancy to trust the dampers on the automatic stabilization system this early in the program. It was; however, just a high speed taxi test.

Things do not always go as planned and the A-12 lifted off the ground at a much lower speed than predicated. As soon as the A-12 became airborne, it was all over the sky. The reason Lou was all over the sky was two fold. Besides the SAS being turned off, the nose gear steering was improperly rigged so that Lou had to pedal in to go straight. This caused a fairly large amount of rudder deflection which, in turn, caused a major side slip as soon as the nose gear came off the ground. Lou then got into a mild pilot induced oscillation, or P.I.O.

Lou Schalk had felt it was not needed to have the Honeywell Stabilization Augmentation System engaged for a high speed taxi run. What wasn't taken into consideration was the very light fuel load needed

The second A-12 built, number 122/06925 spent most of the balance of 1962 perched upside down on the RCS pole at the west central shore line of Groom Lake. The results of this testing helped reduce the overall RCS of the A-12 and SR-71's to less than one tenth of that of current small jet fighters. The Blackbird was the very first of Lockheed's family of stealth airplanes. (Lockheed via Tony Landis)

to taxi the aircraft. The A-12 just wanted to fly. Lou did manage to get the number one A-12 back on the ground, almost causing Kelly to have a heart attack in the process, but nevertheless all in one piece.

When the final design of the A-12 was laid down on paper, every known technique was employed to reduce the radar cross section. The sharp leading and trailing edges of the wing presented a large reflective surface. To reduce this to a minimum, a "sawtooth" design was incorporated on the leading and trailing edges of the wing, chine and control surfaces. The "pie" shaped panels were replaced with radar absorbing composite materials that could withstand the high temperatures encountered during operational flights. This ended up reducing the A-12's radar cross section to about 1/10th that of current small fighters of the early 1960's. The frontal and side RCS was the best with the rear being the worst, but then again who was to catch an airplane traveling at 3,500 feet per second anyway!

Later the A-12 was painted with "Iron Ball" radar absorbing paint over the entire airframe and reinstalled on the RCS pole. The coned tubes extending from the exhaust ejectors were used to emulate the extremely hot exhaust gasses normally being generated by the Pratt & Whitney J-58s. (Lockheed via Tony Landis)

Final check out of the first A-12, number 121/06924, at the east end of building 82 at the Lockheed Skunk Works facility in Burbank, California. The nose assembly has not been installed and the inlet cones are in their fully retracted position. (Lockheed via Tony Landis)

The date of the first official flight, 30 April 1962, was more or less uneventful. A key group of people from the CIA, USAF, Lockheed, Honeywell and Pratt and Whitney were there. The CIA brass got their first look at the Blackbird and were delighted. Probably the most unusual observer at the first flight ceremony, was retired Air Force General,

The A-12s were single seat reconnaissance aircraft, with the sensor systems being controlled by the pilot with the aid of onboard computers. At this point in its final assembly the first A-12 was unpainted. (Lockheed via Tony Landis)

Jimmy Doolittle.

The "official" first flight, piloted by Lockheed Test Pilot Lou Schalk, lasted thirty minutes with a top speed of less than 300 knots. The landing gear was never retracted.

An incident happened on the very first flight right after takeoff, the metal fillets on the bottom of the wing to fuselage mating point began to fly off as Lou accelerated off the Groom Lake runway. This was caused by an opening in the wheel well that allowed ram air pressure to get under and between the wing and fuselage fillets and popping them off. Had the gear been pulled up right away it probably would not have happened until landing.

When Kelly designed the A-12, every effort was made to insure that the aircraft could fly with any of the composite structures missing. Kelly's question was, "What would happen if, let's say, the radome came apart?" Before the material had proven its durability, the design criteria was the aircraft must be flight worthy with the loss of any major part of composite flight controls or fuselage missing at design speeds.

Lockheed did have problems with the plastic rudders. They would absorb moisture and when you got to speed and heated them up the moisture could not escape quickly enough and a build up of steam pressure would pop off chunks of the composite skin.

Early in the flight test program, all flights of the A-12 were J-75 powered and they flew almost a year with that power plant before the J-58's were ready. The beginning of the changeover from the J-75 to the J-58 began on 5 October 1962. To reduce the chance of losing an aircraft by flying an unproven new engine, it was decided to conduct the first flights using the proven and reliable J-75 in the right nacelle and the J-58 in the left nacelle. It wasn't until 15 January 1963, that an A-12 flew with two J-58s.

Lou Schalk makes his first landing on the Groom Lake/Area 51 runway on 26 April 1962. The A-12 was landing to the north with the base POL storage area in the background. (Lockheed via Ken Collins)

The second official flight of the first A-12 (number 121/06924) took place on 30 April 1962. The pilot for the first thirteen flights was the Chief Test Pilot for the Blackbird program, Lou Schalk. In the background is the Papoose Mountain Range just to the West of Groom Lake and Area 51. (Author's Collection)

The first Mach 1 flight occurred on the second official flight, 4 May 1962. The A-12 was programmed to go to Mach 1 as soon as they brought up the gear on the second flight.

During the initial flight test program, the A-12 was flown, on the average, six and a half flights per month. The first Mach 3 flight did not come about until the J-58 power plant had been installed.

It was no problem to reach Mach 2 using the J-58 power plant. It was a different matter with the J-75's. Top speed was about Mach 1.6. Mach 2 was achieved by one of Lockheed's more daring pilots, Bill Park. He flew a J-75 powered A-12 to an altitude of 50,000 feet at Mach 1.6, pushed the nose over into a steep dive and reached Mach 2.

One of the early all J-58 flights will be remembered forever by the flight test team at Groom. One of the flight paths used during the testing program started near Las Vegas, Nevada, went to Wendover, Utah, then

For years it was rumored that some A-12s carried external tanks on top of the inner wing section. They did, but only during engine run up tests and only until the massive fuel leaks were corrected. This A-12 is undergoing engine checks during early March of 1962. The fuel tanks leaked so much in the early testing that the only recourse was to use surplus aircraft fuel tanks mounted externally until the problem was worked out. (Lockheed via Tony Landis)

north-northwest to the Canadian border and return.

On one particular flight on the way back from the Canadian border, something went wrong with an engine or fuel control. The weather was bad and the pilot, Lou Schalk, had to shut down one engine (by this time in the flight testing, many non-navigation instruments had been added). One example were two sets of indicators for the bypass doors. In addition to the two set of switches, there were many manual switches, such as the six hat the pilot had to work manually to keep the each inlet tuned up.

The day this A-12 lost an engine, Lou had to bring it down through the clouds. When the aircraft broke through the clouds, Lou did not know where he was, the only navigation aid that Lou had to determine his location was a ten dollar standby compass. Not really what you want and need when flying a $67 million dollar airplane. It was only with luck and a good sense of direction that Lou and the A-12 finally got home. The next flight, and all subsequent flights, from that time forward had the multiple nav aids installed that were missing on the eventful flight.

The first official Mach 3 flight took place on 20 July 1963. Flown by Lou Schalk, the J-58 powered A-12 reached Mach 3 using a trial and error process.

After reaching Mach 2, each succeeding flight tried to increase the speed by Mach .05. A test fight was flown with a new inlet schedule installed and a new inlet spike profile used with the net result of an engine usually being blown. Back to the drawing board to determine another schedule to try on the inlet spike and the bypass doors. The primary problem turned out to be faulty controls of the spike control system and the need to install "mice" in the inlet to change the subsonic diffusion (flow) angles in the inlet and a need to seal off bleed air from the forward bypass doors. The flight following the sealing of the forward doors was incredible. The aircraft had more acceleration than ever before. The aircraft accelerated so rapidly that they were at programmed speed over Wendover instead of the Canadian border, which was the best to date.

By now the Blackbird was accelerating so fast that Lou had a hard time keeping up with the aircraft. He was busy trimming this and trimming that. Suddenly, at Mach 2.9 or 3, there was a loud explosion. Lou had blown out an engine. Lou thought, "That's all folks, I've bought the farm." After three minutes of being bounced all over the cockpit, Lou managed to get the aircraft under control and head back to the "Ranch".

In all nineteen Blackbirds were lost or written off, eleven SR-71s, two YF-12s and six A-12s. There have been four accidents at Mach 3, two pilots ejected safely; Bill Park in the M-21 number 135, Bill Weaver in an SR-71A number 2004/17953. Unfortunately the two back seaters in these two aircraft did not get out safely. Ray Torriok was the fight test engineer on the M-21 and Jim Zwayer was the RSO in 2004/17953. More on this later.

Of the fifteen A-12s built at the "Skunk Works", seven of the single place birds are still intact. The one and only trainer, 06927, better known as the "Titanium Goose" and one of the two mother aircraft (called the M-21); originally designed to launch the D-21 drone, also remain.

The various models were designed to fill specific roles. The basic A-12 was a single place, Mach 3+ at 90,000 foot reconnaissance platform. As the program moved forward the mission of the A-12 changed drastically from the original design basis. At conception the aircraft's sole mission was to overfly the Soviet Union. On 1 May 1960, Francis Gary Powers was downed and the entire picture changed. Congress passed a law stating, "No manned aircraft over the Soviet Union."

Lockheed test pilot James Eastham takes on fuel for the first time in the number one overall Natural Metal A-12 during early 1963. The KC-135Q was based at Area 51 and used exclusively in support of the OXCART program. The KC-135 is an early short tail variant in overall Natural Metal with DayGlo Orange bands on the nose and tail. (Author's Collection)

OXCART Operations

The criteria established for pilot selection for the men who would fly the A-12 was strict. Obviously the pilots chosen would have to be the cream of the crop. This was due to the overall performance of the A-12 and to the fact that the men had to be cleared to fly highly classified intelligence missions. The pilots had to be between 25 and 40 years old, qualified in the latest high performance aircraft, emotionally stable and highly motivated.

Air Force files were screened for possible candidates and a list of sixteen potential nominees interviewed. The CIA had to go over each and every one's background with a fine toothed comb, followed by a complete head to toe physical. Those that remained were approached to take on employment with the CIA as contract pilots.

When it was all over and done with, eleven pilots passed all the hurdles and were assigned to the 1129th SAS, located at the secret test facility at Groom Lake, or Area 51, in south central Nevada.

When the Groom Lake facility was chosen, it was deficient of most human amenities. The base had inadequate POL storage and the former

An overall Black A-12 (number 132/06938) taxies out for an OXCART training flight from Area 51. Once the program had shut down, this A-12 was moved via truck to its new home at the USS Alabama Museum in Mobile, Alabama. (Author's Collection)

The A-12B trainer moves in toward the refueling boom of a KC-135Q. There was only one A-12B (number 124/06927) built and it was known by the nickname, *Titanium Goose*. The overall Natural Metal aircraft carried the U.S. Air Force logo and national insignia on the port side of the fuselage, but not on the starboard side. The second cockpit was raised to give the pilot forward visibility over the nose. The Goose was the only Blackbird its designer, Kelly Johnson, ever flew in. (Author's Collection)

U-2 runway was woefully deficient in both length and strength. But it did have one thing that no other base had, total isolation. The security was excellent or could be made so, and a moderate construction program could provide sufficient facilities for the OXCART/CYGNUS program.

Lockheed provided a C-47 shuttle service to and from its Burbank location, but daily commuting was out of the question. The team of construction workers were housed in old surplus Navy aluminum trailers, a new water well was dug and a few recreational facilities put together. It would be some twenty years; however, before permanent housing would finally be built at Groom Lake/Area 51.

Three surplus Navy hangars were obtained, dismantled and reassembled on the north side of the base. A handful of Navy houses and barracks were transported from Hawthorne, Nevada and made ready for occupancy by the middle of April 1962 with a full complement of 100 houses in place by the middle of 1963. By early 1962, the fuel (POL) tank farm was ready, with a total capacity of 1,320,000 gallons of what would eventually be called JP-7. During the latter part of 1961, the facility was ready to receive aircraft, but no aircraft arrived until February of 1962.

Aircraft 121 arrived at Groom (as the base was known to those stationed there) on 28 February 1962 with the second A-12, number 122 arriving on 26 June 1962. It spent the next three months upside down on the RCS range pole at the west central edge of the Groom Dry Lake. A-12 number 123 arrived in August and made its first flight in October. The Titanium Goose, the only A-12B trainer, was delivered to Groom in November of 1962. The "Goose," number 124, first flew in January of 1963. The fifth A-12, number 125, arrived at Groom on 17 December 1962.

By the end of 1962, there were two A-12s actively engaged in flight tests, numbers 121 and 123. By 31 December 1962, the two A-12s had reached a top speed of Mach 2.16 at an altitude of 60,000 feet. Still far from the needed Mach 3+ at 80,000 plus feet. The A-12 program suffered from a lack of horsepower or should I say J-58 power. At the end of 1962, all the flights that took place were with one A-12 powered by J-75s and the other with a mix of one J-75 and one J-58. By the end of January 1963, Pratt and Whitney had ten engines available for flight, with the first all J-58 powered flight occurring with A-12 number 121 on 15 January 1963. From that point forward, all A-12 aircraft, with the exception of the "Goose", were fitted with their intended propulsion system. This gave renewed emphasis to the flight test phase and it was expanded to three shifts a day, seven days a week.

On 24 May 1963, CIA pilot Ken Collins ran into a pitot tube icing problem that resulted in A-12 number 123 pitching up, and ending up in an inverted flat spin at 35,000 feet and 600 knots. Ken's only way out was to eject. At the time of the accident, number 123 had completed seventy-nine flights with some 135:20 hours of flight time.

Lockheed test pilots Lou Schalk and Bill Park took the "Goose" up into the same type of weather pattern the very next day and found the problem with ice in the pitot lines. This verified Ken Collins reported failure as their air speed kept increasing falsely.

By the end of 1963, the veil of secrecy was wearing thin. The loss of number 123 near Wendover, UT and the numerous sightings by commercial airline pilots along with the biggest leak by Senator Strom Thurman after he was briefed on the program. That lead up to the announcement of the "A-11" by President Johnson on 29 February 1964. The aircraft he revealed and showed was a YF-12A. On that eventful day, two of the three YF-12s were flown from Groom Lake/Area 51 to Edwards AFB, CA.

The A-12/OXCART program would stay a secret until the official announcement in 1988 that there was indeed a Blackbird that preceded the SR-71 and YF-12; the A-12. This event occurred a remarkable twenty years after the program was terminated.

Three years and seven months after the A-12s first flight, OXCART was declared operational, as it had achieved all of its intended milestones for speed, altitude and endurance.

By the end of 1963, the A-12s flying out of Groom, had accumulated a total of 573 flights, totaling 756 hours of flight time and nine aircraft were in the inventory. On 20 July 1963, Lou Schalk reached Mach 3 for the very first time. He blew an engine in the process and almost lost his life, but he did make it to Mach 3. Again in November of 1963, an A-12 flown by James Easthem, reached the design speed of Mach 3.2, at 78,000 feet. The longest sustained flight at design speed and altitude didn't occur until 4 February 1964, almost two years after the first flight. This time Jim Easthem took number 121 to Mach 3.3 at 83,000 feet for just over ten minutes. Jim was lucky he didn't try for twelve minutes. As it turned out, the wire insulation used in the A-12s were designed for a temperature of 600 degrees F. At Mach 3.3 for ten minutes, the airframe had heated up to over 800 degrees F. When Jim landed after his first 3.3 flight, the cockpit filled with smoke, and there was smoke poring out of every crack and crevasse of number 121. Jim had literally burned all the insulation off all the wiring in the entire aircraft. Another minute or two at design speed would have resulted in the loss of number 121. All the A-12s were grounded for about six weeks while Lockheed replaced all the wiring in all the A-12s.

By the end of 1964, the A-12s had made a total of 1,160 takeoffs and 1,158 landings with 1,616 hours of total flight time. A-12, number 133

This was the Tee Hangar complex built to house the BLACK SHIELD A-12s (followed by SR-71As) at Kadena Air Base, Okinawa, Japan. From this location, A-12s flew operational missions over North Vietnam. On the first mission, the aircraft successfully photographed seventy out of the 190 known surface-to-air missile (SAM) sites in North Vietnam. (USAF via Author)

had been lost on landing at Area 51 on 9 July 1964. Bill Park; now Lockheed's chief test pilot on the A-12 program, had zoomed number 133 to a unofficial record altitude of 96,200. In doing so, Bill damaged the engines and they would not throttle down. Needing to reduce his airspeed for a safe landing, Bill lowered the landing gear. This acted as a speed break and in the process caused the servo actuators to fail due to the thermal shock of the below zero air coming into contact with the super heated hydraulic system through the open wheel wells. This caused a total loss of all hydraulic control. As Bill approached the Groom Lake runway, he lost complete control of his aircraft. His only recourse was to eject at a 45 degree bank at 200 feet just off the south end of Groom Lake runway. Before it's loss, A-12, number 133, had made a total of ten flights and logged 8.19 hours of flight time. It was also the last A-12 off the production line, being delivered in June of 1964.

After flying the A-12s for three years, the total high speed flight time was broken down to; Mach 2.0 (sixty hours), Mach 2.6 (thirty-three hours) and Mach 3 (nine hours). This figure was achieved by flight test aircraft only, no operational A-12s had flown to Mach 3 by the of 1964.

A fourth A-12 was lost at the Groom Lake facility on 23 December 1965, with CIA pilot, Mele Vojvodich at the controls. The A-12, number 126, was lost on takeoff and was totally destroyed. The accident investigation board determined that a flight line electrician had improperly miss-connected the pitch and yaw gyros, and had in effect reversed the controls. Mele ejected safely from an altitude of 150 feet above the frozen Groom Lake which had about four inches of ice on it from the November rains. When Mele left his stricken A-12, his biggest concern was landing in the middle of the fireball of number 126. He didn't, but Bill Park nearly ran him over in the chase car as Bill raced to the scene of the crash. Mele was back on flying status in a matter of a few weeks.

Wanting to see if he could have successfully controlled the stricken A-12; Mele and Lockheed Chief Test pilot, Bill Park, flew to Beale AFB, CA, to recreate the accident on the Air Force's SR-71 flight simulator. They recreated the exact same events that led the to the loss of number 126. Mele tried two or three times to correct for the switched controls, but every single time, he had the same result; he crashed. Bill asked if he could give it a try. After one or two simulated flights, Bill emerged from the SR-71 Flight Simulator with a smile on his face. Mele asked him how he did, and Bill's response was, "No problem, I corrected and over came the problem every time and the rest of the flight was without a hitch." Mele could not believe his ears. With a look of disbelief on Mele's face, Bill could not hold back the laughter. With a big "Gotcha" grin on his face, Bill admitted to Mele, that yes indeed, he had crashed on every takeoff too.

A-12s Declared Operational

On 18 March 1965 Secretary of Defense McNamara and Secretary of State Vance discussed with then CIA Director McClone the increased threat of flying U-2s and drones over The Peoples Republic of China. Several U-2s piloted by National Chinese had already been shot down over mainland China. It was agreed that all necessary steps be taken to operate OXCART over Communist China, flying out of Okinawa. It was at this point that construction began on what was to be called Area 19, at Kadena Air Base, Okinawa. This was the beginning of a reconnaissance program known as BLACK SHIELD. The scenario was to deploy three aircraft to Okinawa accompanied by a contingent of 225 personnel.

With an overseas deployment almost a sure thing, the 1129th SAS (Special Activities Squadron) Detachment 1, began the final validation of OXCART. It set out to demonstrate complete system reliability of all systems at speeds of Mach 3.05 and at a range of 2,300 nautical miles with altitude over target in excess of 76,000 feet. This required three aerial refuelings by different crews flying KC-135Q's. While waiting for the shoe to drop, and the unit to be shipped overseas, training was continued and reliability improved. With longer times at high Mach numbers, new problems began to surface. The most serious problems were electrical in nature. Most related to the connectors to the inlet actuators due to their extremely hostile environment.

This A-12 (number 125/06928) was lost on 5 January 1967 when it ran out of fuel due to a severe fuel tank leak on its way back to Area 51. The CIA contract pilot, Walt Ray, lost his life when the seat malfunctioned after he ejected safely from his stricken A-12 near Caliente, NV. The seat's crew separation sequence jammed and Walt rode the seat all the way in. (Author's Collection)

What, in the author's opinion, has to be the most beautiful airplane ever built, this A-12 (number 128/06931) was restored into the colors and markings of an operational BLACK SHIELD A-12 that flew missions out of Kadena Air Base, Okinawa, Japan between May 1967 and June 1968. They all carried bogus Red tail numbers that were changed before every flight and sometimes the numbers on one side differed from the numbers on the opposite side. This added to the confusion of the North Vietnam spies that operated out of Kadena. On at least two occasions the ground crews used paper stick on numbers that burnt off and the aircraft came back with no tail numbers at all. (Author)

With sustained temperatures in excess of 800 degrees F, together with airframe flexing, severe vibration and shock, it was only a matter of time before wires broke, connectors cracked and insulation wore off.

On 3 August 1965, the Deputy for Technology, John Paragosky, called on Kelly Johnson to address the situation. Measures had to be taken to insure the operational readiness and commitments to BLACK SHIELD be met. In Kelly's typical fashion, he took the "bull" by the horn and arrived at the Groom Lake Facility the very next day to oversee corrective action first hand. Kelly's firm and effective management style had gotten Project BLACK SHIELD back on schedule.

By 20 November 1965, four A-12s were selected and validated for Project BLACK SHIELD, numbers 127, 128, 129 and 131. Of these four aircraft, only A-12 number 128 remained stateside.

After more then a year of waiting to go operational, the 1129th SAS, Det 1, was still at the Groom Lake Test Facility at Area 51. An impressive demonstration of the A-12s capability and a validation as to the mission capability of the A-12, occurred on 21 December 1966. Bill Park, Lockheed's Senior Test pilot flew a 10,198 mile course in just under six hours.

Shortly after Bill had set this impressive unofficial record, a fourth A-12 was lost. While on a routine training flight, A-12, number 125 had been lost near Callente, Navada on 5 January 1967. Walt Ray; one of the CIA pilots, had a problem with a massive fuel leak coupled with a faulty fuel gage, he was trying to return to Groom Lake, when he ran out of fuel at speed. Walt successfully ejected from his disabled craft only to have the seat malfunction. When the accident recovery team found Walt, he was still strapped to his ejection seat. The malfunction was in the crew separation sequence in the seat, and he rode it all the way to the ground. The accident investigation team determined just what had caused the tragic loss and they took steps to insure the same mistake never happened again.

On 17 May 1967, all the waiting and wanting came to an end, the 1129th SAS, Det 1, was being deployed to Kadena, Okinawa. On 22 May 1967, Mele Vojvodich flew, A-12 number 131, non stop from Area 51 to Kadena in six hours and six minutes, some 6,873 miles. A-12 number 127, flown by Jack Layton left Area 51 on 24 May 1967 for a fight to Kadena that took five hours and 55 minutes. Jack Weeks left in A-12 number 129 on 26 May 1967, but suffered INS and communications problems in-route. Under the circumstances, Jack made an unscheduled stop at Wake Island. The emergency recovery team was deployed to secure the A-12 and the flight was resumed the next day without incident. On 29 May 1967, the 1129th SAS, Det 1, was considered operational

It was decided that 31 May would be the big day, OXCART's first operational mission. The moment had arrived which would see the efforts of hundreds of Lockheed, CIA, and contractor personnel and the accumulation of ten years of hard work, missed birthdays, late Christmases and anniversaries come and go. Was it worth the cost in human terms? Was it worth all the worry? The answer from all involved was a resound "YES". As fate would have it, the morning of the 31 May dawned with a heavy rain. No OXCART aircraft had ever flown in heavy rain before. Since the weather over the target area was clear, and the time was nearing for a commitment to be made; the decision was made that the mission was a go. With Mele Vojvodich at the controls OXCART launched the first mission into history.

This first mission lasted three hours and thirty-nine minutes. The speed over target, North Vietnam, was Mach 3.10 at 80,000 feet. The mission results showed that Mele had photographed seventy of the known 190 SAM sites in North Vietnam and nine primary targets. The mission was deemed a success! Between the time of its very first mission on 31 May 1967 and the last approved operational mission on 8

This is the finest example of a restored A-12 cockpit that can be seen today. This beautiful example of 1950s technology can be found at the Minnesota Air Guard Museum in St. Paul, Minnesota. This A-12 (number 128/06931) is on public display on week ends from the middle of April to the end of September. (Author)

May 1996, a total of twenty-nine operational missions were flown.

The end of BLACK SHIELD was coming, the replacement for the A-12, the Air Force/Lockheed SR-71A was in place and ready to take over the helm of strategic reconnaissance The SR-71 would never fly as high or go as fast or ever take better photographs, but the time of the CIA having its own air force was coming to a close. On 16 May 1968, the Secretary of Defense, Clark Clifford reaffirmed the original decision to terminate OXCART and store the aircraft at Air Force Plant 42, Site 2. On 21 May 1968, President Lyndon B. Johnson confirmed Secretary Clifford's decision.

Project Headquarters selected 8 June 1968, as the earliest possible date to begin redeployment of the A-12s back to Area 51. Meantime, flights for the three A-12s at Kadena were to be limited to those essential for maintaining flying safety and pilot proficiency. After returning stateside, they would proceed into storage, joining the balance of the A-12 fleet.

During its last flight before returning to the U.S., A-12, number 129, piloted by Jack Weeks was lost. Jack's body was never recovered, nor was any trace of number 129 ever found.

The program lasted just over ten years, from conception to termination. A summary of the program highlights follows:

The first flight by Lou Schalk was on 26 April 1962.

First J-75/J-58 flight by Lou was on 5 October 1962.

First J-58 only flight was on 13 January 1963.

First Mach 3 flight by Lou was on 20 July 1963.

First sustained Mach 3 flight by Jim Eastham took place in November of 1963.

First sustained Mach 3.2 flight occurred on 3 February 1964, flown by Jim Eastham.

An A-12 achieved a top speed of Mach 3.29 and an altitude of 90,000 feet with a sustained flight time above Mach 3.2 of one hour and fourteen minutes, piloted by Bill Park on 20 November 1965.

Longest flight of an A-12 flown by Bill Park on 21 December 1966. The flight lasted just under six hours and covered a record 10,198 miles.

Highest any Blackbird ever flew; 96,250 feet in A-12 number 133, on 9 July 1964. The pilot was Bill Park and the aircraft was lost on the same flight.

The fastest any Blackbird has ever flown was A-12 number 128, the KIAS was indicated at 538 knots (red line was 500 KIAS). This happened during flight test and the Mach was reported to be Mach 3.56. An SR-71 flown by Ben Bowels flew to a top speed of Mach 3.43, again during flight test. Operational A-12s were limited to Mach 3.3, with SR-71s being limited to Mach 3.2, but usually flown at only Mach 2.8.

The first A-12, number 131 was flown to Kadena in six hours and six minutes on 22 May 1967. The aircraft was flown by Mele Vojvodich.

First operational A-12 mission flown over North Vietnam on 31 May 1967, the pilot was Mele Vojvodich.

First and only Blackbird ever to sustain flak damage was on 30 October 1967. The aircraft, A-12 number 129 was flown by Denny Sullivan.

Last operational mission flown in support of BLACK SHIELD was on 8 May 1968. The A-12 was number 131 and it was piloted by Frank Murray.

The last A-12 to fly was number 131 transiting from Area 51, Groom Lake to Air Force Plant 42, Site 2, on 21 June 1968. Flight time was 55 minutes, at an altitude of 30,000 with a max speed of Mach 1.06. This aircraft was flown by Frank Murray.

Lockheed built and flew fifteen A-12s, of these six were lost, with the remaining nine assigned to museums. One of the finest examples of the A-12s on public display is the Minnesota Air National Guard Museum's A-12, number 128, located at the Minneapolis-St. Paul International Airport. The other is the sole remaining M/D-21 at the Museum Of Flight, located at Boeing Field, Seattle, Washington.

In a ceremony at the Groom Lake Test Facility, at Area 51; Vice Admiral Rufus L. Taylor, Deputy Director of the CIA, presented the CIA Intelligence Star of Valor to pilots Kenneth S. Collins, Ronald (Jack) L. Layton, Francis J. Murray, Dennis B. Sullivan and Mele Vojvodich for their participation in the BLACK SHIELD Operation. The widow of Jack W. Weeks accepted his award posthumously.

This is Air Force Plant 42, Site 2, Palmdale, California, final resting place for a number of A-12s. In the center is the overhaul facility for all Blackbirds, A-12, YF-12s and SR-71s. Nine A-12s are visible in the outside storage area at the left of the hangar. (Author)

YF-12A Improved Manned Interceptor

From the advent of interceptor development, most advances had been characterized by a series of small, incremental improvements. The performance of each new interceptor exceeded that if its predecessor by tenths of a Mach number, a few thousand feet in altitude and small increases in overall combat radius. The weapons followed the same path, very small and sometimes difficult to identify increases in range, performance, kill probability and sensor type. All the while being heavily dependent upon the close control provided by the ground radar environment. The Lockheed/USAF YF-12A took a giant leap forward in both capability and independent operation.

The almost airtight security that surrounded the production and early flight test of the YF-12A generated some misconceptions as to its mission and how it would be employed. The weapons system was designed to accomplish the defense of the continental United States of America and Canada using a completely different concept of operations from the 1960's Air Defense Command scenario.

The AF-12, as the YF-12A was called early in the program, came into being in September of 1960. It was the product of a proposal to the Air Force to build a long range, very high speed interceptor to address newly perceived Soviet threats. During late October of 1960, the Air Force sent a letter of intent along with a check for one million dollars instructing Lockheed to proceed with Plan 3A, the commitment for production of three AF-12 interceptors. The number seven A-12 was ear marked to be modified into the AF-12 prototype.

The AF-12, as conceived by the Lockheed design team, would utilize as much of the Lockheed/CIA A-12 airframe and systems as possible. It would incorporate the Hughes ASG-18 fire control system originally developed for the canceled North American Aviation F-108 Rapier. The Fire Control Officer's position would occupy the "Q" bay area of the A-12 that was normally used for camera systems. A separate project group was assembled to develop, integrate and build the AF-12 from the on going A-12/OXCART program. The Northwest corner of the "Skunk Works" main building; Building 310; was cordoned off from the rest of the production facility. On 23 and 24 January 1961, Lockheed had its first meeting with the Air Force's weapon system project office that would over see the AF-12 AN/ASG-18 weapons platform.

The first flight of the number one YF-12A (number 1001/06934) ends as the aircraft lands at the south end of Area 51's north/south runway with Lockheed Test pilot James Eastham at the controls on 7 August 1963. The Air Force instructed Lockheed to air brush out the mountains in the background so no one would know the YF-12 was landing at Groom Lake, Nevada. (Lockheed via Tony Landis)

The first photograph ever released of the first YF-12 was given out on 29 February 1964. This was the only evidence that the U.S. Air Force had a Mach 3 aircraft until its first public showing in September of 1964. (Marry Isham Collection)

On 31 May 1961, the Air Force reviewed the progress of the AF-12 program and reviewed the status of the AF-12 mock-up. All parties came away from the meeting pleased with the programs progress. By June, the wind tunnel models revealed directional stability problems that were a result of the modified nose radome, chine cutback (required for the very large Hughes developed forty-eight inch pulse Doppler antenna used with the AN/ASG-18 fire control system) and the newly revised and raised cockpit canopies of the AF-12 design. For the first time, ventral fins were added to the underside of the engine nacelles and a folding, non-movable centerline fin was added on the underside of the AF-12's rear fuselage.

Throughout the Summer of 1962, Kelly Johnson continued to work on both the A-12 and AF-12 programs simultaneously. This was a very tasking project for Kelly as each program was mutually exclusive of each other in both mission and security considerations.

The AN/ASG-18 fire control system posed a new problem for Kelly and the AF-12 design team, no one had ever fired an air-to-air, or ground-to-air missile from a platform traveling in excess of 3,300 feet per second.

Furthermore, no one seemed to be in agreement as to how to go about doing just that. On paper, it seemed at least that it could be done and wind tunnel tests confirmed the basic design philosophy, but only by actually going out and doing the impossible, could the engineers prove their ideas to be correct.

By 3 August 1963, all the funding and re-allocation of the seventh through ninth A-12 airframes for modification to the AF-12 configuration had been cleared and approved by all members of the Air Force, CIA and the Lockheed design teams. By this time, all the major struc-

The first YF-12 on one of the test ramps at Area 51 on 8 October 1962. It required vast amounts of ground support and test equipment in order to properly evaluate the tremendous performance of the Lockheed YF-12. This area of the Groom Lake test facility was in the northwestern end of the Area 51 complex. (Author's Collection)

The number one YF-12A (1001/06934) on the taxiway at Area 51. The streamlined pods mounted under the engine nacelles are camera pods and there was one on each side to photograph the release and launch of the Hughes AIM-47 air-to-air missile. Unlike the high explosive airborne weapons of today, the Hughes AIM-47 carried a 250 kiloton nuclear warhead. (Author's Collection)

tural pieces for the second AF-12 had been positioned in the production tooling jigs and the first AF-12, Lockheed build number, 1001, was being reassembled at the Groom Lake Test Facility or, Area 51, for its first flight.

On 7 August 1963 the first AF-12 made its first fight with Lockheed test pilot, James Eastham at the controls. Kelly Johnson made a comment shortly after the first fight that, "It is the first airplane I've ever worked on where the fire control system was checked out prior to the first flight."

With the announcement by President Johnson on 29 February 1964 of the existence of the "A-11" Advanced Manned Interceptor, the cloak of secrecy partially came off the AF-12, now given a proper Air Force designation of YF-12A. Just prior to the Presidents announcement of the "A-11", the first two YF-12As, numbers 1001 and 1002, were flown from the Groom Lake Test Facility, to Edwards AFB, California. In their haste to conceal the two YF-12As from public view, Lou Schalk and Jim Eastham made a direct approach and landing on Edwards main runway, taxied directly to the awaiting hangars, where they were pushed in tail first and the doors closed. The twin YF-12As were still very hot from the subsonic dash from Area 51 to Edwards, that the heat from the massive P&W J-58's set off the hangar deluge system and just about drowned some of the ground support crew.

On 16 April 1964, the first XAIM-47 air-to-air missile was ejected

A Lockheed employed ground crewman moves in to place the wheel chocks as the number one YF-l2 comes to stop. The fire truck had followed the YF-12 in from the end of the runway as a precaution. (Marty Isham)

A highly retouched view of YF-12A number 1001/06934, at the run up pad just east of the main runway at Area 51. The mountains, normally visible in the background, have been airbrushed out to hide the aircraft's true location. (Lockheed via Tony Landis)

There was no public viewing of the first two YF-l2s (tail numbers 06934 and 06935) when they flew in from the Groom Lake test facility at Area 51 to Edwards AFB, California on the morning of 29 February 1964. It was not until 30 September 1964 that the press got their first view of the Blackbirds and even then the press wasn't allowed to photograph them or take notes. There was a mad scramble to write down every thing they could remember once they were back on the bus. (Marty Isham)

The first YF-12 on the ramp at Edwards Air Force Base, California with the forward weapons bay doors and both cockpit canopies in the open position. The aircraft has a pair of Red remove before flight banners on the pitot tube. (Marty Isham)

The number one YF-12A was painted overall Black and carried an Air Defense Command badge on the port fin and an Air Force Systems Command badge on the starboard fin. These badges were self adhesive decals and burnt off after the next high speed run. (Marty Isham)

The first YF-12A takes off on the main Edwards runway for a test flight. The nose landing gear rotates forward and the main landing gear rotates inward. All markings and lettering were in White. (Marty Isham)

from the YF-12A in flight. The missile was an inert launch verification shape, but it did prove that you could launch a missile from an aircraft traveling at over 3,300 feet per second, or Mach 3+. There was a problem with the angle that the XAIM-47 left the YF-12A; however, and had it been a live firing, it would have passed through the cockpit.

On 9 January 1965, Lockheed YF-12 test pilot, James Eastham had taken YF-12A, number 1001 out to Mach 3.23, sustaining Mach 3.0 for five minutes. Three months later, on 18 March 1965, YF-12A number 1001 would fire its first live AIM-47 against a flying target thirty-six miles away with a closure rate of over 2,000 mph. Kelly wrote in his log "We are scheduled to fire against many drones, including these at low altitude."

On 1 May 1965, the first and third YF-12As, flown by Air Force crews set three absolute world speed records. Aircraft number 1001: straight course 2,070. 101 mph at an Absolute Sustained Altitude of 80,257.65 feet. The aircraft was flown by Colonel Robert (Fox) Stevens with Lieutenant Colonel Daniel Andre as his back seater. Aircraft number 1003: closed course speed of 1,688.889 mph. Flown by Lieutenant Colonel Walter Daniel, with Major James Cooney. The third record was also set by aircraft number 1003: 500 km course 1,643.041 mph, flown by Lieutenant Colonel Walter Daniel and Major Noel T. Warner.

The YF-12A program took a closer step to production on 14 May 1965, when the Air Force funded a $500,000 contract for engineering on

The production line for all the YF-I2A's was confined to the north west corner of the Lockheed Skunk Works building 309/310. This YF-12A, under construction on 23 August 1963, was the second of three YF-12s (number 1002/06935). The aircraft made its first flight on 26 November 1963 with Lou Schalk at the controls. (Marty Isham)

The YF-12A production line was totally separate from the A-12 OXCART production line and it took a different security badge to enter either line. This made "Show and Tell" visits from congressional types who wanted access to the Blackbird but were, not cleared to see the A-12, somewhat easier. (Author's Collection)

The frame outside the YF-12A production area was the framed structure that was used to cover all the Blackbirds for movement from Burbank to Area 51 at Groom Lake (for the A-12s) or to Palmdale (YF-12As and, later, all SR-71s). (Author's Collection)

Looking south along the spine of the YF-12A in its separate production area, the entire A-12 production line comes into view. (Author's Collection)

the follow-on F-12B. This would have been the operational configuration of the YF-12A. The capabilities were similar with the only major visible change being a modified chilled radome. No production go ahead was given, but it did look encouraging for a go ahead in the near future.

Meanwhile the flight testing of the Hughes AIM-47, AN/ASG-18 pulse Doppler fire control system continued on track. On 9 September 1965, a GAR-9 (AIM-47) was fired from the number one YF-12A while flying at 75,000 feet at Mach 3.2. Kelly was again delighted with the performance of his aircraft and wrote in his daily log that the program was "Hitting the high speed corner of the design program." The missile came within six feet six inches at a range of thirty-six miles with the tar-

The number two YF-12A on the ramp at Groom Lake (Area 51) looking north with a view of the dry lake in the background. The aircraft was a mixture of Natural Metal and Black paint at this point in the flight test program. (Author's Collection)

The second YF-12A (number 1002/06935) prepares for a test flight from Groom Lake/Aera 51 with Jim Eastham in the cockpit. (Author's Collection)

The cut back chine and large radome on the YF-12A made it easy to identify it from all other Blackbird variants. The YF-12 remains the fastest interceptor to ever fly in USAF service.

One of the key identification features of the YF-12A was the cut back chine and large radome. The number two aircraft was parked on the ramp at Area 51, from this one can easily see why the site was selected for secret testing, there is absolute nothingness in the background. (Author's Collection)

The second YF-12A taxies down the Edwards ramp for a day of flight testing. At this point in its flying career, YF-12, 1002/06935, carried a White stenciled Air Force Systems Command badge on both vertical fins. (Marty Isham)

The third and final YF-12A (1003/06936) made its first flight on 13 March 1964 from Area 51 with Lockheed Test pilot Bob Gilliland at the controls. Later the aircraft was transferred to Edwards Air Force Base for further testing. (Author's Collections)

get drone flying at an altitude of 40,000 feet, "which is a very good shot." On 10 November 1965, a third installment of one half million dollars was awarded Lockheed for further F-12B design work in order to keep the program alive. At the same time, a Summary of JCS Recommendations on the Draft Presidential Memorandum and Related Secretary of Defense Actions for FY66 stated the following: "The Secretary recommended provisions of $5 million for further development of the YF-12A advanced interceptor which is now undergoing tests. The JCS recommended approval of pre-production funds for the F-12A to retain the option of deploying an advanced interceptor at the earliest date. The Secretary of Defense's plan does not provide for such preproduction funds, but does retain the option to deploy this interceptor in the future if it is decided to do so."

Flight testing had now reached a point where the Air Force was ready to test the YF-12As Hughes AN/ASG-18 pulse Doppler fire control system against realistic targets in hard to track and detect environments.

The number three YF-12A (1003/06936) is prepared for a run for the speed record on 1 May 1965. A close examination will show almost twenty technicians in or near the YF-12 prior to engine start. (Marty Isham)

Ground crew prepare to start engines on the number three YF-12A prior to one of its record runs on 1 May 1965. One of the ground crew moves the air starter hose to the starboard engine nacelle. (Lockheed)

Colonel Robert (Silver Fox) Stephens and Lieutenant Colonel Daniel Andre in the number one YF-12A (1001/06934) just prior to their record speed and altitude run on 1 May 1965. They established a record of 80,258 feet at a speed of 2,070.12 miles per hour. (Marty Isham)

The third YF-12A was used in the speed record runs over a closed course on 1 May 1965. The large White cross on the underside of this Blackbird was used by ground station cameras to verify speed over the course. (Marty Isham)

The operational cockpit of the second YF-12A Advanced Manned Interceptor (1002/06935). There are vertical instruments on either side of the artificial horizon, the one on the left is a speed indicator in both Mach number and knots, the one on the right is an altimeter. (Lockheed via Tony Landis)

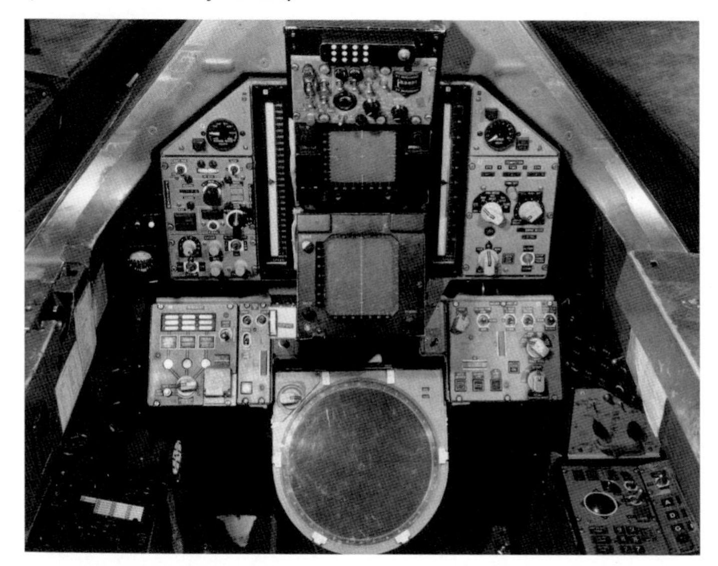

The only photo ever released of the back seat cockpit of the YF-12A with a ASG/18 Hughes fire control system prior to NASA modifying it for flight test. (Lockheed via Tony Landis)

The number three YF-12A (1003/06936) taxies out to begin world record speed flights on 1 May 1965. (Marty Isham)

The Hughes AIM-47 (left) and the prototype XAIM-54A Phoenix missile (right). The primary difference between the two missiles was that the AIM-47 uses a 250 kiloton nuclear warhead and had a semi-active seeker while the AIM-54A has a fully active seeker and uses conventional type explosives in its warhead. (Hughes)

On 25 April 1966, two YF-12A aircraft, numbers 1001 and 1003, were flown to Eglin AFB, Florida, where they would seek, track and fire on a variety of aircraft. The day the YF-12As arrived was to be a major milestone for the program. Aircraft number 1001, flying at an altitude of 75,000 feet at Mach 3.20 fired at a Boeing QB-47 flying 60,000 feet below the YF-12A. The pilot, Jim Eastham, fired an unarmed AIM-47 at the oncoming QB-47. The missile passed through the QB-47s horizontal stabilizer taking some four feet of control surface with it. If the AIM-47 had been armed, the QB-47 would have been destroyed. The mission was considered a complete success. During the six months and seven firings, the YF-12As weapon system scored an impressive six out of seven direct hits, with the one miss attributed to a missile gyro system failure.

In the month of July, Kelly Johnson wrote in his log, "We were directed to give up further flying of the YF-12As, although we had proposed shooting down a drone at Holloman to get the effects of ground clutter for low altitude targets."

By August of 1967 Kelly had laid off half of the YF-12A test force crew, retaining just enough personnel to put the YF-12As in storage, either at Palmdale, Edwards, or back at the Skunk Works in Burbank.

The decision to follow on with the F-12B came and went and by Christmas of 1967, the call came down from the SPO. The Air Defense system for which the F-12B would be built was going to be canceled. The only portion of the program that would remain intact were items directly related to the vulnerability study which was to be transferred to

The number three YF-I2A (1003/06936) carried three world records on White YF-12 silhouettes on the nose. (Tony Landis)

the SR-71. On 5 January 1968, a formal order was issued "closing down the F-12B" with the YF-12A being canceled as of 1 February 1968. The cancellation notice on both the fighter programs included a letter to Kelly Johnson instructing Lockheed to destroy the A-12/F-12 and SR-71 tooling. Kelly's parting comment to this order was, "We have proceeded to store such items as are required for production of spare parts at Norton. The large jigs have been cut up for scrap and we are finishing the clean-up of the complete area. Ten years from now the country will be very sorry for making this decision of stopping production of the whole Mach 3 series of aircraft in the USA." The scrapped tooling was sold for seven cents a pound to local scrap dealers.

After the cancellation of the F-12B and YF-12A programs with the Air Force, three YF-12s were put into flyable storage. The Air Force had indicated to NASA that they could be made available to NASA to be used for research. The details were worked out and an agreement was reached with the Air Force and formalized in a letter of understanding.

The radome has been removed from the number two YF-12A so that the radar could be serviced. The Hughes ASG/18 radar used a huge dish for both search and track. The underfuselage weapons bay is open. There is a camera mounted on the canopy framing of the front canopy that filmed the instrument panel during flight. (Author's Collection)

A refueling boom operators view of a YF-I2A as it comes in to take on fuel from a KC-135Q high over the Mojave Desert of Southern California. (Marty Isham)

This letter was signed on 5 June 1969, with a public announcement being made of the transfer on 18 June. The text of the memorandum stated that the Air Force would make two YF-12As, personnel and facilities available to the program, and NASA would pay for the operational expenses. Aircraft numbers 1002 and 1003 were turned over to NASA.

NASA planned to use its newly acquired stable of twin Blackbirds as research tools, test beds and guinea pigs to test a whole range of experiments. The airframe, propulsion system and other systems in the aircraft were of the type NASA would have expected to see in a Mach 3 aircraft, whether it was military or commercial. The YF-12As operational hardware with its fixed configuration, structural design and systems made it the ideal workhorse for high speed research. It was to be used to evaluate the state of the art in many areas of theoretical aerodynamics, structural predictions and performance predictions to name but a few. It was to be used in the correlation of data with what they knew at the time from theoretical predictions and wind tunnel predictions.

The twin titanium canopies were built to withstand the heat of Mach three flight and provide protection to the crew. The Red and White triangle is the ejection seat warning marking. All warning notices were painted in White. (Author's Collection)

A NASA pilot prepares for a flight in the modified YF-12A (1002/06935. The aircraft was modified with static tubes mounted at an angle of 45 degree off the canopy center line. (Tony Landis)

(Above & Below) The equipment bays are lowered on the NASA YF-12A (1002/06935) on the NASA ramp at the Ames Research Center. These pallets were lowered on cables which were located at each corner, and along the sides of the pallet. In their lowered position, each was easily accessible to ground crews and servicing technicians. (Tony Landis)

The primary objective of the NASA program was to provide baseline information at high speed and at high altitude conditions so they could assess the theories as they apply to high speed aircraft design.

The overall NASA YF-12 research program was directed out of NASA Headquarters and managed out of the Edwards Flight Research Center. There were contributions from NASA's Langley, Lewis and Ames Research Centers in addition to the Flight Research Center. Langley was interested in fundamental aerodynamic experiments and advanced structural test panels; Lewis was interested in propulsion systems aspects in both theory and in wind tunnel testing areas; Ames' primary interest was in wind tunnel testing and various theoretical aspects, as well as some of the simulation aspects. The Flight Research Center's task was to tie it all together through the aircraft ground and flight tests. Lockheed was contracted to provided the expertise in systems, flight operations, administration and also provided past history research data and design history. In addition, all flight test plans were reviewed by Lockheed.

The first task at hand on receiving actual physical control of the YF-12As, was to install instrumentation in the form of strain gages and thermocouple instrumentation. The wing and fuselage of the YF-12As were instrumented for aerodynamic loads. Three stations on the wing and about three locations on the fuselage were set up for strain gauges. The left side of the aircraft were instrumented for the measurement of temperatures to define the thermal environment that the aircraft actually experienced. The first flights were to set base line data and these went on for about a year. Lockheed aero and propulsion engineering groups provided NASA with years of experience to keep NASA from having to re-do all the initial flights. Once the airborne data line was established, NASA put the YF-12s through a series of tests in the High Temperature Loads Laboratory located at NASA/Edwards. The objective was to measure flight loads with the combined effect of temperature and load and then attempt to separate them by running it through the laboratory tests. Lockheed also provided the wind tunnel models and supported wind tunnel testing.

A lousy rainy day on the NASA/Dryden ramp as ground crews prepare the NASA YF-I2A, 1002/06935 for a day of test flying. The equipment bay pallets are lowered to allow access for servicing. (Tony Landis)

One of the contributions of the YF-12 program was that NASA now had instrumentation and procedures that would allow the industry to make those measurements on hot airplanes.

The YF-12A flight test program continued at a modest pace using the number two YF-12A, number 1002. The Air Force had been utilizing the number three YF-12A, number 1003 for a series of tests where it was being used to simulate the Russian MiG-25 Foxbat (a Mach 3 dash capable fighter/interceptor) at various speeds and altitudes. The ASG/18 radar was kept operational by a team of Hughes engineers. On its sixty-third flight on 24 June 1971, the third built YF-12A, while on final

A full size mock-up of the operational F-12B was displayed for USAF officials on 6 July 1964 as part of the aircraft's final design review of the F-12B configuration. By utilizing a chimed radome the F-12B eliminated the need to have the foldable center line ventral fin or the fixed small ventral fins under the nacelles that were used on the YF-12As. (Author's Collection)

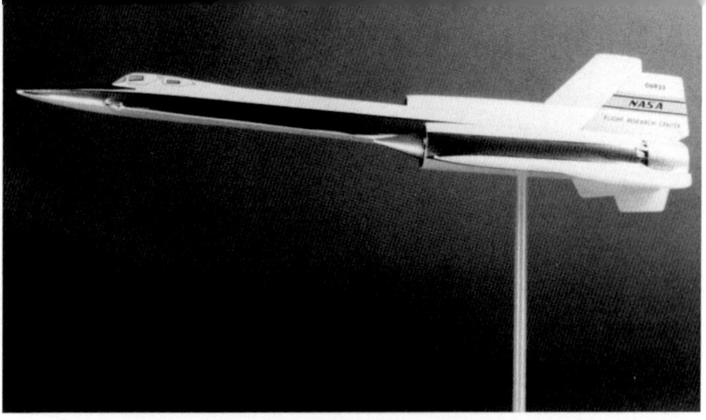

Over the years there were rumors of an overall White SR-71 or YF-12. The closest these ever came to reality was a 1/72nd scale model painted in the proposed scheme. The overall aircraft was White, the NASA band is standard Yellow and Black with Insignia Blue panels running the entire length of the aircraft with Black pin stripes on the top and bottom of the Blue band. A Flat Black anti-glare panel was incorporated in front of the wind screen. The main reason this configuation never actually flew was that it would have been an absolute nightmare to keep clean. (Author's Collection

approach, experienced a major inflight fire in its right engine nacelle caused by the failure of a major fuel line. The fire was uncontrollable and the crew; pilot, LTC Ronald (Jack) Layton and FCO, Major Billy Curtis, were forced to eject at low altitude. This basically ended the Air Force portion of the program. The aircraft crashed about 3.5 miles northeast of the Edwards Air Force Base north boundary and was totally destroyed. A month after the loss of 1003, the Air Force agreed to loan NASA the second production SR-71A, number 2002, serial 61-7951. The stipulation was that NASA could not refer to the SR-71A as such and a cover (bogus) designation and bogus serial number was attached to the SR-71A. From that point forward, number 2002 was referred to as the YF-12C serial 6006937 (this serial number had in fact been assigned to an A-12, number 131, the very last A-12 to fly).

In the early part of 1977, the two YF-12s had completed more than 175 flights. A good percentage of these flights were at or above Mach 3.0. But the cost of flying two high performance aircraft became too much for NASA to justify. Costs of the YF-12 program were harder to justify in a shrinking budget environment. In the Spring of 1977, a decision was made by NASA to retire the YF-12A and to return the YF-12C (SR-71A) to the Air Force. A year after the decision to wind down operations, the YF-12C was returned to the Air Force on 27 October 1978 and put into storage at Air Force Plant 42, Site 2, the resting place of the nine remaining A-12s. The sole remaining YF-12A made its 146th and final flight to the Air Force Museum on 7 November 1979. With this came an end to the world's first and only Mach 3+ fighter. The program did have a number of spin offs; the Phoenix missile system used on the Navy/Grumman F-14 is a derivative of the original Hughes AN/ASG-18 pulse Doppler fire control system proven on the YF-12s.

An early scale model of a proposed NASA hypersonic research drone mounted on the upper fuselage of the YF-12C/SR-71A (2002/17951). The idea was that the Blackbird would carry the drone to Mach 3, then it would be released to fly a pre-programmed research mission at hypersonic speeds. (Author's Collection)

The NASA/Ames Research Center studied the YF-12A as a possible platform for testing advanced engines and propulsion systems and other high speed concepts using wind tunnel models such as this one. (Author's Collection)

A one twelfth scale model of the YF-12A is readied for testing in the Ames Research Center's nine foot by seven foot supersonic wind tunnel. (Tony Landis)

Three of the Lockheed Skunk Works finest designs. The upper aircraft is the NASA YF-12C/SR-71A, (2002/17951), the lead is a NASA F-104G Starfighter and the lower aircraft is YF-12A 1002/06935, with the "Cold Wall" tube on the centerline. The YF-12C/SR-71 is easily identified by its fully chined nose. (Tony Landis)

The NASA YF-12A (1002/06935) parked on the ramp with the weapon bays open and a special equipment rack extended from the left rear weapons bay. In addition to its NASA tail band, the aircraft still retains its national insignia and full USAF markings. (Tony Landis)

(Right) This YF-12A (1002/06935) carried the "Cold Wall" tube mounted on the fuselage underside on the centerline of the airframe. In addition, the aircraft had a specially modified static pitot tube used to measure very minute side slips and other micro movements of the YF-12A while in flight. (Tony Landis)

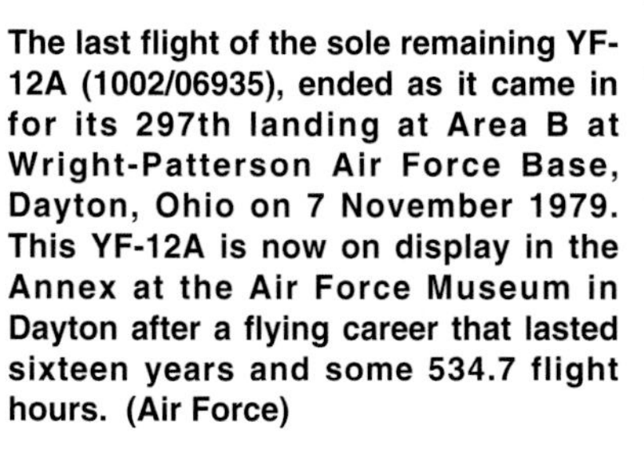

The last flight of the sole remaining YF-12A (1002/06935), ended as it came in for its 297th landing at Area B at Wright-Patterson Air Force Base, Dayton, Ohio on 7 November 1979. This YF-12A is now on display in the Annex at the Air Force Museum in Dayton after a flying career that lasted sixteen years and some 534.7 flight hours. (Air Force)

TAGBOARD/SENIOR BOWL, The D-21 Drone

The least known of the Lockheed Blackbirds was the D-21 supersonic drone. This vehicle grew out of the need for an unmanned reconnaissance platform to overfly the Soviet Union and China. Developed under the same survival requirements as its famous big brother, the A-12/SR-71, the D-21 had to be able to cruise at 90,000 feet and Mach 3.5.

When conceived, in the early part of 1958, the A-12s primary mission was to overfly Soviet airspace. With the downing of Francis Gary Powers on 1 May 1960, the rules of the game changed. One of the many concessions for the release of Powers was a promise made by President Eisenhower for the immediate cessation of all manned, repeat, manned overflights of the USSR. With our satellite capability to cover Soviet and Chinese activities still a good eighteen to thirty-six months away and still an unknown quantity at that time, the process was put in motion in early 1960 to build an unmanned vehicle, which would become known as the D-21.

The original A-12 was now in full production. Not wanting to develop two completely new systems simultaneously, Lockheed and the CIA attempted to make the most out of what was known about Mach 3 flight.

The vehicle had to be simple, relatively light weight, capable of Mach 3.5 flight at 90,000 feet, have a low radar cross section, and be compatible with systems already under development. One of the first decisions was to continue with the double delta or ogival delta wing design used on the A-12. Because of weight restrictions and the complex design of the inlet and associated hardware, the Pratt and Whitney J-58 power plant, a turbo-ramjet, was dropped from consideration.

Lockheed was not totally unfamiliar with other types of power plants. They had successfully initiated the Lockheed X-7 program on 8 December 1946. The purpose of this program was to develop a family of unmanned research vehicles to test aerodynamic and propulsion systems at very high speeds. Like the D-21, this unique airplane was developed by the Lockheed Skunk works.

The basic mission of the X-7 was to serve as a supersonic and hypersonic ramjet test bed, specifically, for power plant development for the USAF/Boeing IM-99 Bomarc anti-aircraft missile. A secondary mission was to use a fully instrumented X-7 to explore aerodynamics, thermodynamics, special fuels and materials for future projects.

At one time, during the development of the A-12 and the D-21, the concept of using boron slurries or boron high energy fuels was considered. Based on tests made with the X-7 on at least three different occasions, the prospects looked promising. The overriding considerations

This was the Q-12 prototype mockup. The production D-21 drone differed very little from this mockup. (Lockheed via Tony Landis)

with the use of Boron based fuels was the difficulties in the transportation and handling of these exotic fuels. The Boron fuels, themselves, were very toxic. Vapors with a concentration of only a few parts per million of the fuels were deadly if inhaled. To make handling and transportation that more difficult, the fuels were capable of spontaneous combustion.

With its foundation built on the information gathered on the X-7 program and their close working relationship with the Marquardt company, the program began to take shape in the Fall of 1962.

The power plant for the D-21 (originally referred to as the (Q-12) was a Marquardt RJ43-MA-20-B4 ramjet. The first Dash 11 engine, as it was called, was used on the USAF/Boeing Bomarc IM99B. First flown in September of 1959, the Dash 11 engine was flight qualified in August of 1960. From the beginning of production in August of 1960 through the end of the production run in October of 1962, the Marquardt Company produced a total of 656 Dash 11 engines. For applications in the USAF/Boeing Bomarc IM-99B, the fuel used was standard JP-4 with an estimated design point operational performance of Mach 2.7 at 70,000 feet. The upper envelope limit for an unmodified Dash 11 engine was 85,000 feet at Mach 3.2.

With this information and the resulting X-7 data, Lockheed asked Marquardt to redesign the exhaust ejector while ADP redesigned the inlet system to permit higher sustained Mach numbers. The only other change was the decision to use JP-7 and triethylborane (TRB) as the ignitor so that all Blackbirds used similar fuels. This required a re-jetting of the fuel nozzle ring, due to the differences in fuel characteristics and the installation of the chemical (TEB) ignitor system.

Once the propulsion system decision was finalized, the launch platform needed to be addressed. From the birth of the D-21 program, it had been decided that a modified A-12 (now called the M-21) aircraft would be the mother aircraft. Ram jets do not begin to function until the

The first A-12/M-21 (center, number 134/ 06940) was under construction at the Burbank Skunk Works production facility in Building 309/310 on 23 August 1963. (Author's Collection)

For the first mating of the Q-12 (D-21) drone to the M-21 mother bird, the drone was moved from its production line in building 82 under the cover of darkness to building 309/310 and mated to the M-21. Much to everyone's surprise, it fit on the very first try. (Lockheed via Tony Landis)

The first M-21 (number 134/06940) on the ramp at Area 51. Number 134 never did actually launch a D-21 drone, but was used for captive flights and as the photo chase for the four launches from the other M-21, number 135/06941. The sole remaining M-21/D-21 is now on display at the Museum of Flight at Boeing Field, Seattle, Washington. (Author's Collection)

This was one of the first photos of the M/D-21 released by the CIA during 1982. The aircraft was M-21 number 134/06940 and the mission was one of the first captive flight test which took place some eighteen years earlier on 22 December 1964. (Lookheed/CIA)

The M-21 mother ship (134/06940) on the ramp at Area 51 with a D-21 in place on the fuselage centerline pylon. This ramp is located just east of the main north-south runway which is on the south shore line of Groom Dry Lake. (Author's Collection)

speed approaches Mach 2.2. The A-12 should be able to fly at Mach 3.25 with a D-21 on its back. Computer models (crude by today's standards) were developed and wind tunnel tests were run to establish the proper angles and geometry necessary for such a combination. All that had to be done was to find a way to separate a forty-three foot long, nineteen foot wide, 11,500 pound drone from a "Mother" aircraft traveling at Mach 3.2 and at 80,000 feet without incident.

The D-21 was situated between the vertical stabilizers of the M-21 mother airplane. From the wing tip of the D-21 to the innermost edge of the M-21 tail was a scant six inches, not much room for error at these speeds.

The mating and adjusting of flight characteristics proceeded with a minimum of problems. The D-21 was placed to the rear of the normal center of gravity and a little nose high. To reduce the drag of an open non-functioning inlet to a minimum, jettisonable nose and tail cones were installed on the first captive flights. The after body flaring took on an almost identical shape to the extended tail cone of the SR-71. The inlet cover was angled down to assist the airflow over the M-21 and D-21 and reduce drag at high Mach numbers.

The first captive flight of the D-21 on the M-21 occurred on the same date of the first flight of the SR-71, 22 December 1964. The target date, in 1965, for the first launch was to be on Kelly Johnson's birthday, 27 February. A year later, and many problems behind them, the first launch had still not taken place. Finally on 5 March 1966, some twelve and a half months after the first planned launch, a successful launch of a D-21 from the M-21 took place. The location was over the Pacific Ocean between Point Mugu and Vandenburg AFB. This location was chosen to take advantage of the tracking facilities and restricted airspace of the Vandenburg range.

Unlike the original A-12s, the M-21 aircraft carried a pilot and a sec-

The first flight of the M/D-21 with Bill Park at the controls took place on 22 December 1964. The pair flew over the frozen Nevada landscape with Lockheed Test pilot Art Peterson flying chase in a Lockheed F-104G Starfighter. (Lockheed)

When the M/D-21 TAGBOARD program came to an end on 30 July 1966 the remaining D-21s were modified to the D-21B configuration for launch from Boeing B-52H Stratofortresses. (Author's Collection)

The first production D-21 (number 501) undergoes modification to D-21B standards in the modification bay of building 82 at the Lockheed Skunk Works facility at the Hollywood Burbank Airport. (Author's Collection)

The first D-21B (airframe number 501) undergoes modification during May of 1967. The vehicle was later lost when a bolt failed and it fell from the wing pylon of the B-52H launch aircraft. The aircraft crashed somewhere between Riverside and Palm Springs, California. (Author's Collection)

The drone required a booster rocket to get it up to operating speeds. The elevons and rudder have been removed and the vehicle is resting on a specially built transport dolly. (Author's Collection)

ond crew member, the Launch Control Officer. His job was to monitor the "Daughter" (D-21) and with the aid of a periscope, visually confirm the separation of the inlet cone and observe the separation of the two "Blackbirds".

On the first attempted launch, the separation of the inlet and tail cone assembly proved to be a major stumbling block with the result being the almost total destruction of the D-21's leading edges and the ingestion of FOD (Foreign Object Damage) into the inlet, damaging the ramjet. From that fight and all subsequent flights, the D-21s were flown without the cones and the D-21 was powered up at Mach 1.24 inflight to help eliminate drag and to assist the M-21 in accelerating to design speed and launch altitude. Fuel used by the D-21 during this portion of the flight was replenished from the fuel reserves of the "Mother" ship.

The M/D-21 combination was not as simple as one might seem. The added weight of the D-21 made getting to the launch point a real challenge. To be at speed and altitude over the Pacific Missile Range, the M/D-21 had to start it's speed run over Albuquerque, New Mexico. The hope was that the M-21 would not run out of fuel before it reached 80,000 feet at Mach 3.27.

Once the Marquardt Dash 20 ramjet was powered up and design speed and launch point was reached, the M-21 was flown into a .9 G arc to assist in D-21 separation. The key to a successful launch required the D-21's thrust to be equal to the mother aircraft's forward thrust. Both aircraft had to be at or near the c/g neutral point. With the D-21 at a normally neutral attitude, and the M-21 in a .9 G arc, the natural direction would be straight up and out, missing the twin rudders on either side. At Mach 3.25, the other item that had to be taken into account, was that the D-21 would sustain an "Unstart" as it passed through the bow wake of

The D-21 was extremely large for an unmanned vehicle. There are five Lockheed technicians standing on top of the fuselage of number 501, with plenty of room to spare. The vehicle number was painted on the nose in White. (Author's Collection)

The seventh D-21B is placed into the modification jig in Building 82. The wings, fin, engine and other systems have been removed for overhaul and modification. The windows in the underside are for cameras mounted in the reconnaissance bay. (Author's Collection)

This D-21, number 501, has its two step intake shook cone removed, along with the wings and all composite surfaces. (Author's Collection)

Number 501 has had the fin and rudder reinstalled although the vehicle is still minus its ramjet power plant. The diamond shaped object in the middle of the tail assembly is part of the tail support stand that kept the D-21 from falling on its tail. (Author's Collection)

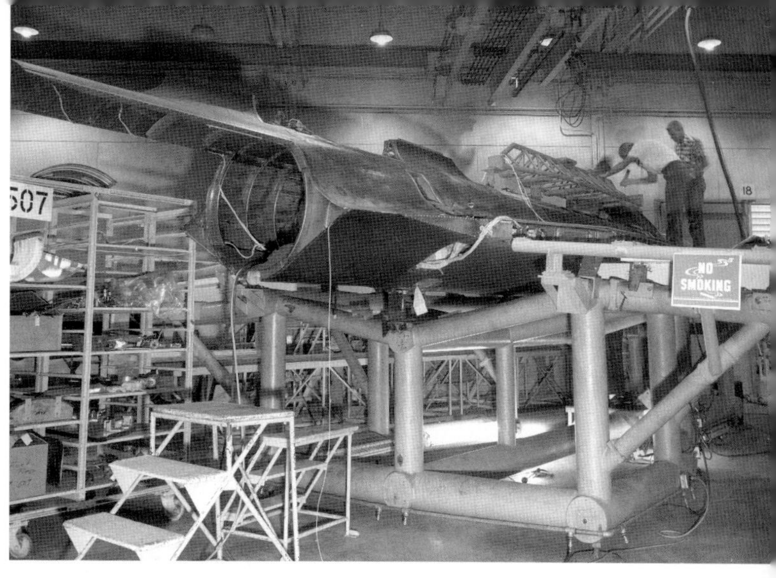

The seventh D-21B, number 507, sits snugly in the modifications jig so that Lockheed technicians can perform the necessary work changing this drone from a M-21 launched vehicle to one that will be carried by a B-52H. (Author's Collection)

Number 501 has had its ramjet power plant reinstalled. The long arm attached to the tail assembly is part of the tail support stand which kept the tail heavy D-21 from falling on its tail. The discoloration of the ram jet ejector indicates that this engine has been run. (Author's Collection)

A D-21B main fuselage structure with the engine, control surfaces and composite pieces removed is suspened from a work jig. The long intake ducting is visible in the nose section. (Author's Collection)

A row of D-21s on vehicle support dollies undergoing modification to D-21B standards. Front to rear, D-21s number 507, 510 (in Natural Metal), 509, 511 and 508 (in background). (Author's Collection)

D-21s stacked up like a cord of wood awaiting their turn in the modification center. The inlet shock cones have been removed and most have been stripped of their Black paint. (Author's Collection)

This was the camera bay hatch of a D-21B with the camera windows removed. The camera bay was the heart of the D-21 system. (Author's Collection)

The aft section of the D-21B with the engine removed reveals the internal structure of the rear fuselage and rudder hinge points. (Author's Collection)

the M-21. To overcome this problem, a Platinum catalytic screen was installed aft of the flame holder of the ramjet, to assist in the re-light of the motor.

From its first successful launch from the M-21 on 5 March 1966 with a twenty-five percent fuel load, Lockheed completed two additional launches. The second was on 27 April 1966 with a fifty percent fuel load and the third, a heavy weight launch, on 16 June. The flight on 16 June was the most successful to date, flying almost 1,600 nautical miles and making eight programmed turns.

Kelly had asked Bill Park whether or not he thought the operational pilots could hold a .9 G arc in a combat situation, Bill didn't think so, as it was very difficult to hold to that profile under ideal conditions. It was decided that the next launch; one with a full fuel load would be made at one G.

The D-21 systems were checked out and the launch sequence began. As the D-21 passed through the M-21's bow wake, it experienced an "asymmetrical unstart" situation. This is where the flame holder looses the right or left side of the fuel burn, causing the D-21, number 504, to roll to the right at separation. As a result, the M-21 pitched up uncontrollable and Bill, feeling the pitch up, pushed the control stick full nose

A line-up of four reconnaissance/camera bay hatches resting in modification jigs. The reconnaissance bay was the only part of the D-21 that would be recovered after the vehicle flew a successful mission. (Author's Collection)

This modified D-21B reconnaissance bay hatch was used on a D-21B that photographed the separation of the drone from the B-52H Stratofortress launch aircraft. The Natural Metal fairing was the housing for the movie camera. (Author's Collection)

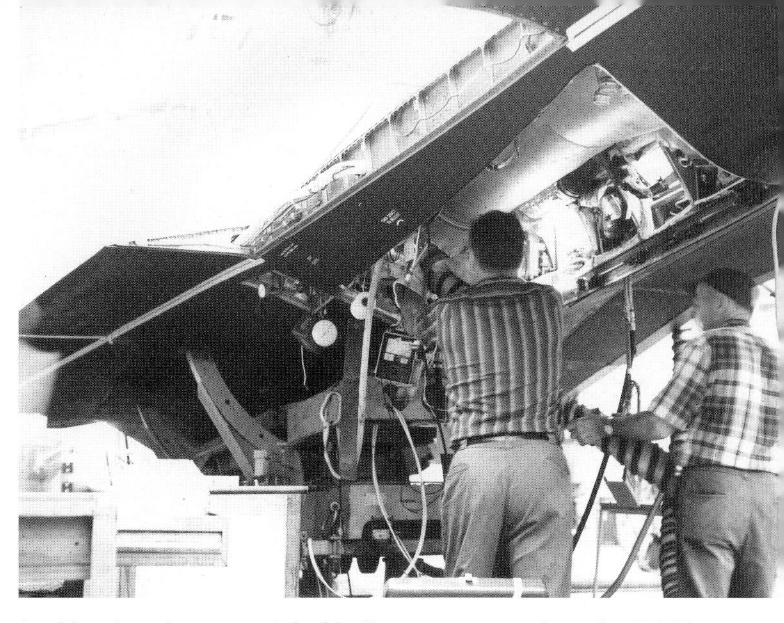

Lockheed engineers work inside the open camera bay of a D-21B drone. (Author's Collection)

The Boeing B-52H Senior Bowl mounting pylon being readied for mating to a D-21B drone for the first time on 1 June 1967. The B-52H Senior Bowl would carry two D-21Bs and their boosters on the same mounting points that had been used to carry the North American Aviation Hound Dog air breathing cruise missile. (Author's Collection)

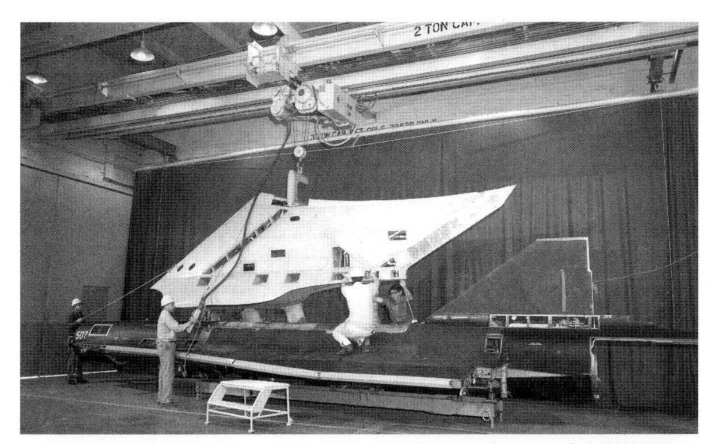

A Lockheed engineer works on the electrical wiring of D-21B number 507 while the vehicle rests on its transporter trailer. The ram jet engine has been removed for maintenance. (Author's Collection)

This was the reconnaissance bay (without cameras) of the D-21B drone. There was not much room in the bay for anything other than was absolutely necessary for the mission. The tube running from front to rear was the air inlet duct for the Marquardt MA43-RJ20-S4 ram jet engine. (Author's Collection)

The Lockheed Missile and Space Division developed the D-21B rocket booster. This booster is mounted on a transport dolly as Lockheed engineers attach the nose fairing. (Author's Collection)

A D-21B booster assembly rests on its transporter dolly prior to having the nose fairing installed. The booster had a five degree downward tilt to the exhaust nozzle. (Author's Collection)

Lockheed technicians work on assembling a D-21B booster nose cone prior to the installation of the Ram Air Turbine or RAT, which would be installed at the extreme end of the nose cone. (Author's Collection)

The D-21B booster nose cone assembly with the Ram Air Turbine (RAT) covered in tape prior to being attached to the main booster assembly. (Author's Collection)

down, literally jamming the control stick into the forward instrument panel. Before the D-21 (number 504) had time to get out of the way, the D-21 and the "Mother Ship" collided in mid-air. The D-21 took out the right rudder, right engine nacelle and most of the right outer wing panel, followed by the M-21 breaking apart just forward of fuselage station number 715.

The Launch Control Officer, Ray Toriek, unfortunately lost his life, not in the flaming crash, but by drowning in the Pacific after successfully bailing out at 40,000 feet. Miraculously, Bill Park, Lockheed's Chief Test Pilot, survived. Bill Park had another problem to contend with when he punched out over the vast Pacific -- drowning. If it were not for the quick actions of the para-rescue team and a lot of luck, he would have lost his life by drowning after surviving a midair collision at 80,000 feet.

As a result of the loss of one of only two M-21s, the program was terminated in early August of 1966, with the USAF/Boeing B-52H becoming the preferred launch platform. The sole remaining M-21, number 134, Air Force serial 60-06940, never did launch a D-21, but was used for captive flights of the D-21 and used for photo chase during the four launches. Bill Park was the only pilot to launch the D-21 with the job of Launch Control Officer being shared between Lockheed Flight Test Engineers, Ray Torick and Keith Bethwick.

The final section of the D-21B booster was the rear fairing. The fin folds to the right for takeoffs and landings when the vehicle is attached to the Boeing B-52H mother ship. (Author's Collection)

A D-21B rocket booster assembly is pulled from its cold soak tube prior to a test firing. The cold soak tube was used to bring the booster temperature down to minus 55 degrees F to simulate an altitude of 40,000 feet, which would be a typical altitude for a B-52H mission. The booster was cold soaked for some ten hours to simulate a full mission profile. (Author's Collection)

SENIOR BOWL

The next segment of the D-21s life centered around SACs main stay, the eight engined, 488,000 pound strategic bomber, the B-52H. As with the "Mother/Daughter" combination; the B-52/D-21B flight tests were conducted out of Area 51.

The B-52H was the only aircraft capable of carrying two D-21s (gross weight of each D-21B with booster was 34,000 pounds) on what appeared to look like two modified X-15 pylons. This marriage proved to be the one that eventually went operational. This combination was first flown on 28 November 1967 with two D-21s, numbers 508 and 509. After months of extensive flight testing and various levels of success and failures, the B-52H/D-21B was considered operational with the 4200nd Support Squadron, which was based at Beale AFB, California, from the latter part of 1969 to its last operational launch on 30 March 1971.

The B-52H had to be modified for the D-21 mission. An observation blister was added to either side of the fuselage. This was for verification of drop and ignition of the solid fuel booster rocket. In addition to the standard complement of crew, the special B-52Hs carried a team of contractor and CIA personnel that were needed for launch control and system support.

The D-21B needed a booster to bring the ramjet up to operational speeds; generally around Mach 3.35. A very large external booster, 30.16 inches in diameter and 44.25 feet long; designed and manufactured by the Lockheed Missile and Space Division; was attached to the D-21 at the M-21 mounting points on the bottom of the drone.

The M/D-21 combination did not require the stand off range of the B-52H/D-21B; nor did it require a booster stage to propel it to the higher Mach numbers for proper ignition of the ramjet.

The M/D-21 had a radar signature of less than twenty-four square inches while the signature of a B-52H was almost 200 square feet. The small signature along with the Mach 3.25 speed and an operational altitude above 85,000 feet made the M/D-21 immune to Soviet or Chinese air defenses. The B-52H/D-21B, on the other hand, flew low and slow and was a very big target.

The thoroughly cold soaked booster is prepared for ignition at the Santa Cruz mountain test range some 100 miles south of San Francisco by a team of engineers from the Lockheed Missile and Space Division. This division of Lockheed is located in Sunnyvale, California. (Author's Collection)

This was the first photograph released by the CIA of the Senior Bowl B-52/D-21B combination. The Stratofortress was moving in to take on fuel from a KC-135A. (Author via Lockheed/CIA)

A team of Lockheed technicians work to mate a B-52 launch pylon and a D-21B drone at the Lockheed Skunk Works on 1 June 1967. (Author's Collection)

The final mating of the launch pylon and the D-21B took place at the Lockheed Skunk Works, Building 82 on 1 June 1967. (Author's Collection)

The B-52H/D-21B launch pylon was completely manufactured at the Lockheed Skunk Works facility at AF Plant 42, Palmdale, California. The plyon was specifically designed to take advantage of existing hard points within the wing of the B-52H mother ship. (Author's Collection)

A Boeing B-52H Stratofortress (serial 61-0021) is readied for installation of the Senior Bowl D-21Bs launch pylon under the inner wing, The pylon is visible on the transporter dolly to the rear of the B-52H wing. The mating took place at Area 51 on 6 June 1967. (Author's Collection)

A line-up of Blackbirds on the ramp at the Groom Lake Test Facility, Area 51, also known as The Ranch and Dreamland to name just a few of the nicknames for the facility. The first aircraft in line is the number one A-12, the second aircraft is the only A-12B two seat trainer variant, it is followed by six more A-12s. The last two Blackbirds are the first two production YF-12As. The mountains in the background are the Whiteside Mountains and Freedom Ridge. (CIA via John Andrews)

This was the first released photo of an A-12. It was cleared for release by the CIA during 1982. This was A-12 number 129/06932, which was lost near the Philippine Islands on 5 June 1968. CIA contract pilot Jack Weeks lost his life when the aircraft apparently disintegrated at high Mach, just one flight short of being rotated back to Area 51. (CIA via John Andrews)

(Right) The only A-12B in the fleet, number 124/08927, sits on the taxi way at Area 51 in the Groom Lake Test Facility. The trainer was affectionately called the *Titanium Goose* and was the only Blackbird Kelly Johnson ever flew in. It was flown solely with Pratt & Whitney J-75 engines and never received the overall Black paint scheme that the rest of the A-12s carried. (Authors Collection)

Parked in front of the CYNGUS/OXCART hangars at the south end of Area 51 this A-12, number 130/06933, sports its very distinctive Natural Metal and Black paint scheme. This A-12 now resides on a specially built pylon at the entrance to the San Diego Museum of Flight at Balboa Park, San Diego, California. (Author's Collection)

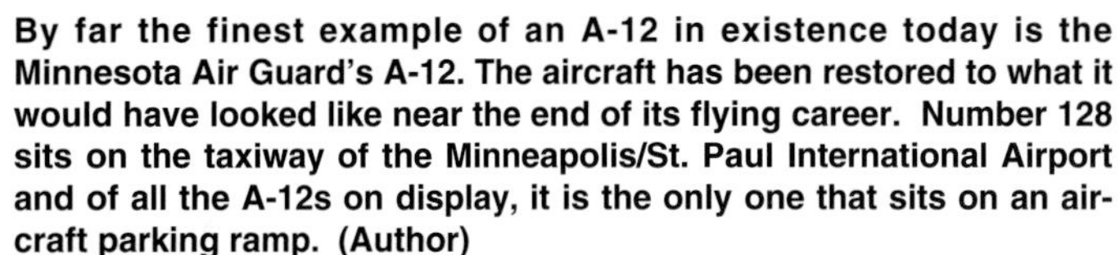

By far the finest example of an A-12 in existence today is the Minnesota Air Guard's A-12. The aircraft has been restored to what it would have looked like near the end of its flying career. Number 128 sits on the taxiway of the Minneapolis/St. Paul International Airport and of all the A-12s on display, it is the only one that sits on an aircraft parking ramp. (Author)

With the launch pylon secured to the wing hard point, Lockheed technicians added weight to the pylon structure to verify the structural integrity and strength of the pylon assembly. (Author's Collection)

Operational sorties for the B-52H/D-21B were flown out of two locations: Area 51 at the Groom Lake Test Facility and Beale AFB, California. With only one known exception, no other facility saw this combination. The exception was the modification depot at Air Force Plant 42, Site 2, Palmdale, California. B-52H/D-21Bs based out of Beale AFB, would air launch over the Hawaiian Island of Hilo, or between Hilo and Midway Island for flights over the Peoples Republic of China. Aircraft based out of Beale AFB, could go anywhere in the world, with proper tanker support, that the mission requirements dictated it to go.

On 9 November 1969, the first operational D-21 mission took place from Beale AFB. The bomber made a rendezvous with a KC-135A, (also out of Beale) over the western Pacific. Heading on a track due west, a second refueling was made with an Eielson based KC-135A from the 6th Strategic Wing, Det 1 out of Shemya AFB, Alaska, over the Central Pacific. Carrying the D-21, the B-52H was close to or at its

This was the D-21B launch control panel inside the B-52H. (Author's Collection)

Additional weight was added to the pylon assembly to simulate the weight of the D-21B drone and its booster. (Author's Collection)

maximum gross weight. The systems operator made final evaluation of the D-21 sensors and phase two began.

The target was an area where construction of ICBM facilities were believed to be ongoing west of Lop Nor, China. The flight path of the D-21 was 900 miles due west of launch point. The on board Honeywell navigation system kept the D-21B right on the money. At Mach 3.3 at

This was the right side of the launch control panel which was located in the former EW position in the upper crew compartment of the Boeing B-52H. (Author's Collection)

Hanging from the port pylon of a B-52H, this D-21B (number 501) and booster, carries ten inch high Gloss White numbers on either side of the air intake and on either side of the rear fin and rudder assembly. The nose numbers are approximately six inches back from the front edge of the inlet opening and six inches up from the leading edge of the chine centerline. (Lockheed via Tony Landis)

The B-52H Senior Bowl aircraft was capable of carrying and launching two D-21Bs on separate mission profiles. The White tip on the D-21B booster was the propeller for the Ram Air Turbine (RAT). (Lockheed via Tony Landis)

A Boeing B-52H Senior Bowl Mother ship (serial 61-0021) carrying a pair of D-21Bs (one under each wing). The Stratofortress carried Vietnam era camouflage. (Lockheed via Tony Landis)

90,000, the fuel consumption was close to that of other A-12/SR-71 type aircraft. The auto navigation system would trigger the cameras to start rolling at the precise moment the target came into view. With the mission complete, the easy part was now over. The D-21B had to bring its valuable cargo home for the analysts at the CIA to evaluate. To accomplish this, the recon bay, INS, Auto pilot and navigation system had to be recovered intact. As it turned out, the first operational mission did not succeed, since the D-21B never came back.

The on-board navigation computer was to have vectored the D-21B to a point off the southwest coast of the Hawaiian Islands for an aerial recovery. A special JC-130 team was dispatched from Hickam AFB, for the pick-up, while a recovery ship had been in the area for several hours.

Of the four operational missions launched against mainland China, the first never came back. The second launch, on 16 December 1970, returned to the recovery point, but the recon bay capsule was never recovered. The third mission on 4 March 1971 was successful, but "Murphy's Law" prevented the recovery of the recon bay capsule and it was lost at sea. On 20 March 1971 the fourth and final mission was

The final resting place for the D-21Bs is Davis-Montan Air Force Base. Of the seventeen D-21Bs at Davis-Montan, NASA will get four (two for flight testing and two for spare parts), the Air Force Museum has received one, the Smithsonian Air and Space Museum and the Museum of Flight at Boeing Field, just south of downtown Seattle, Washington, each got one. The balance of the D-21Bs may go to various museums around the country during 1996 and 1997. (R.J. Archer)

A YF-12A (number 1001/06934) flies on a westerly course over the California high desert near the Edwards Air Force Base flight testing complex. The Blackbird has the folding centerline ventral fin deployed. The aircraft is also equipped with a pair of streamlined bullet shaped camera pods mounted under the air intakes. (Marty Isham)

The second YF-12A in flight over the California high desert just west of Edwards Air Force Base. This YF-12A carries an Air Force Outstanding Unit Award badge painted on the fin above the White tail numbers along with a stenciled Air Force Systems Command badge. (Lockheed via Tony Landis)

This is the first YF-12A number 1001/06934. Many views of this aircraft have been seen and they were all taken on the same day. The Blackbird carried the Air Defense Command badge on the port fin, which was an off the shelf self-adhesive decal. On the next high speed flight, the decal burned off, as did the Air Force Systems Command badge decal that was placed on the starboard fin. (Marty Isham)

The second YF-I2A (number 1002/06935) on the ramp at the NASA/Dryden Flight Test Facility at Edwards AFB, California. The twin Buick engine start cart is just to the outside edge of the port wing, the parachute door on the aircraft spine is open and the rear canopy and seat are missing. This YF-12A carried the older style NASA fin band in Yellow just below the White tail numbers. (Tony Landis Collection)

The Hughes AIM-47 air-to-air long range missile, the forerunner to the highly successful AIM-54 Phoenix system used on the Navy F-14 Tomcat. The missile was on a transporter parked next to the number three YF-12A at Edwards. The aircraft carries three missile launch markings in White on the nose. (Author's Collection)

A formation of Lockheed fighters, the leader is a Lockheed F-104G Starfighter in NASA marking, the aircraft in the foreground is the NASA YF-12C/SR-71A number 2002/06937, while the Blackbird in the background is the second YF-12A, 1002/06935 (which carried a bogus serial number, actually assigned to A-12 number 131/06937), with the "Cold Wall" tube extended. (Tony Landis Collection)

A NASA F-104G Starfighter, number 811, carrying Orange and Yellow markings flies chase for the number two YF-12A (1002/06935) after it was assigned to NASA. (Marty Isham)

YF-12A, 1002/06935 begins its turn onto the final leg for entering the Edwards AFB complex landing approach pattern. The aircraft carries a White circle with a cross in it on the bottom of its port wing. This was a photographic reference symbol and was also carried on the top of the port wing. The markings are used for photographic calibration as was the White dashed stripe running almost the entire length of the outboard engine nacelle. (Author's Collection)

The third YF-12A (1003/06936) was used in the speed record runs over a closed course on 1 May 1965. The large White cross on the bottom of this Blackbird is used by ground station cameras to verify its speed over the course. The aircraft set two records, one at 1,688.889 mph (closed course) and another of 1,643.041 mph (500 km closed course). (Marty Isham)

A Pratt & Whitney J-58 turbojet undergoes testing on a test stand at Beale Air Force Base, California. The rear section of the engine becomes nearly translucent after running for forty-five minutes at full military power. (Pratt & Whitney)

This D-21B is mounted on a M-21 "Mother Ship" at the Museum of Flight, located at Boeing Field, just south of Seattle, Washington. (Author)

flown. It too was a failure. It was assumed that the D-21B encountered very heavy air defenses and was shot down on its final leg of the return flight.

If any of the missions had been successful and the recon package had been recovered intact, the D-21B was to be destroyed by a command destruct from the JC-130 pick up aircraft. The next phase would have been the immediate removal and processing of the photographic sensor's payload. This was to be done at Hickam AFB, by members of the 4200nd Support Squadron. Once processed and analyzed, the information would have been dispatched to the requesting agencies. Sensor information could be on the desk of an analyst in the CIA within twenty-four hours of its initial collection.

With the agreement negotiated by President Nixon of the Peacetime Aerial Reconnaissance Program (PARPRO Treaty) in 1971, and the gradual normalization of relations between the U.S. and the Peoples Republic of China; these wonders of Kelly's "Skunk works" were no longer needed and TAGBOARD/SENIOR BOWL was taken out of service for good.

The D-21 program should not be considered a failure, just the opposite. It took high speed unmanned flight where it had never been before with a minimum of manpower and fanfare, all the while pushing the envelope the whole way.

With storage space at Norton Air Force Base becoming increasingly scarce, the decision was made, in 1975, to remove the D-21s from Norton and deliver them to the aircraft storage and disposal center at Davis-Monthan Air Force Base at Tucson, AZ. The D-21Bs were airlifted to Davis-Monthan in Lockheed C-5As and transported under armed guard to their storage site during the Summer of 1976.

In the twenty or so years that the D-21s have basked in the Arizona sun, they have only been viewed and photographed by the public on a few rare occasions. The first time was in December of 1976; the second, almost five years later to the day, on 5 December 1981. And the third time was in the Summer of 1992, by Popular Science's West Coast Editor, Stu Brown. Other then these three times, access to these; the most obscure of Lockheed's Blackbirds; has been severely limited. At full count there were seventeen aircraft remaining out of the thirty-eight D-21s built.

Their full story has been a long time coming. Kelly Johnson said in February of 1982, at a banquet presentation to the engineers of the Avionics Division of Honeywell; that the, "CIA had reevaluated the security status of this program. They were going to reclassify the program upward, with the declassification date not coming until the year 2011." Well Kelly's prediction proved to be wrong. In the Fall of 1993, the first D-21 arrived at the Air Force Museum and on 20 January 1994, D-21 number 503, was mounted on top of the sole remaining M-21 at the Museum of Flight, Boeing Field in Seattle, Washington. Four D-21s are going to NASA for high speed and NASP testing, with the balance of the D-21s going to various museums around the country.

The Museum of Flight's D-21/M-21 is displayed in full operational markings. The M-21 is in Natural Metal and Black, while the D-21 is in overall Black with White markings. (Author)

The square panel in the underside of the D-21 is where the reconnaissance bay was located. This bay was ejected during the recovery phase and was the only portion of the D-21 that was to be recovered after a mission. (Author)

The D-21 fit snugly between the vertical fins of the M-21 "Mother Ship" with a slightly upward tilt to assist in separation. The D-21 is number 503, the third vehicle built. (Author)

SENIOR CROWN, The SR-71 Blackbird

The SR-71 program has been covered fairly well over the years beginning with Lou Drendel's "Blackbirds in action" which was first released in 1981, as well as several other books and publications.

The Lockheed/USAF SR-71 was the shining jewel in the SENIOR CROWN program for twenty-five years of operational service; from its first flight on 22 December 1964 until its last official record breaking retirement flight on 6 March 1990 (although the term retirement may prove to be premature). No other weapons system could match the performance, technological breakthroughs or just plain awesome presence that the SR-71 Blackbird could bring to any public gathering. Even today, when someone sees any one of the twenty-five Blackbirds that are now in museums, it is still a sight to behold.

During the course of the last thirty years that I 'have been gathering information and data on the Blackbird family of aircraft, the men and women that worked on the bird everyday, the pilots that flew this wonder of Kelly Johnson's "Skunk Works", from their first encounter to their last, all looked at this titanium beast with awe.

As the A-12 program began so did the ground work for what would eventually become the SR-71. As early as April of 1962 and just prior to the first flight of the A-12, the Skunk Works was working on a proposed two seat manned reconnaissance/strike version of the single seat A-12 that would address the specific needs of the U.S. Air Force.

After a number of different proposals, configurations, visits and meetings with various senior Air Force and SAC personnel, the Air Force, on 18 February 1963 authorized the initial construction of the first six SR-71 aircraft with the understanding that a contract for twenty-five additional aircraft would be issued by 1 July 1963.

What was unusual for this initial order of six SR-71s for the Air Force was the means by which the order was processed, it came through the same organization that gave us the U-2 and the A-12, the Central Intelligence Agency. This proved to be a double edged sword for the A-12/Oxcart program. By sharing the tooling, R & D and unit cost with the Air Force, it brought down the overall cost of the A-12 to just over 47 million dollars, guaranteed the Air Force a reconnaissance aircraft follow on program to the CIAs and in effect, killed the A-12 program in the process.

The new aircraft was referred to early on as the R-12, a reconfigured A-12 that was slightly stretched and structurally strengthened to accommodate additional fuel and a second crew member. The "Q" bay which had housed the very capable Itek camera system was now going to be the location of a second cockpit which housed the Reconnaissance System Officer, better know as the RSO. With the elimination of the

The SR-71A forward fuselage fabrication area on 24 July 1964. In the background, behind the White wall was the final YF-12A (1003/06936) which was undergoing its final checkout. To the right of the YF-12 area was the final M-21 (number 135/06941). (Lockheed via Author)

A SR-71A forward fuselage being built up in the fixturing jigs. Directly behind the SR-71A station is the last of three YF-12As to be completed at the Lockheed Skunk Works. (Lockheed via Author)

Lockheed technicians work on a SR-71A in the outer wing panel and engine nacelle fabrication area of building 309/310 at the Lockheed Skunk Works on 21 July 1964. (Lockheed via Author)

A D/M-21 combination moves in to take on fuel from a KC-135Q tanker high over the Nevada desert. The D-21 was designed to fly reconnaissance missions over Red China and the Soviet Union, since Congress had passed a law stating that there could be no *manned* missions over either country. (Lockheed)

Carrying a D-21 drone above the fuselage, this M-21 mother ship (number 134/06940) climbs for altitude over Area 51. (Lockheed via Tony Landis).

A D-21 drone mounted on the upper fuselage of the M-21 mother ship. The drone rode between the twin vertical fins. This was just prior to the first captive test flight on 22 December 1964. (Lockheed)

(Left) A B-52H takes on fuel over southern California while carrying a D-21B on the underwing pylon. The long object under the drone was the booster rocket needed to get the drone up to the proper speed needed to ignite the ramjet engine. (Lockheed via Tony Landis)

The SR-71 production line at the Lockheed *Skunk Works*, Burbank, California with five SR-71s in various stages of completion during mid-1965. During this time, this was probably one of the most highly classified locations in the entire country. There were very few people in the country outside the intelligence community that knew of the aircraft or its outstanding reconnaissance capabilities. (Lockheed via Author)

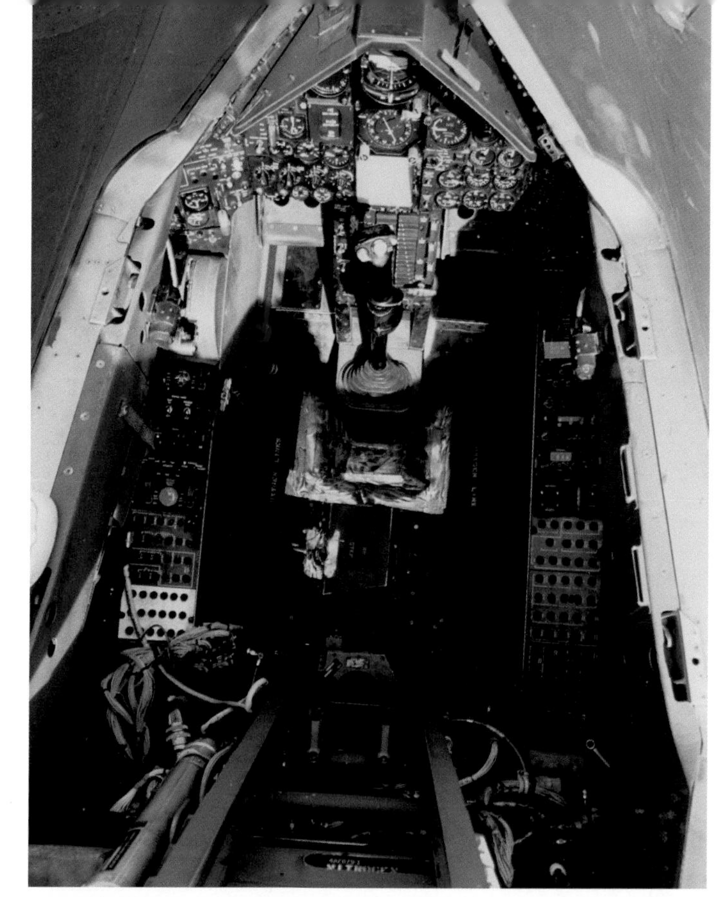

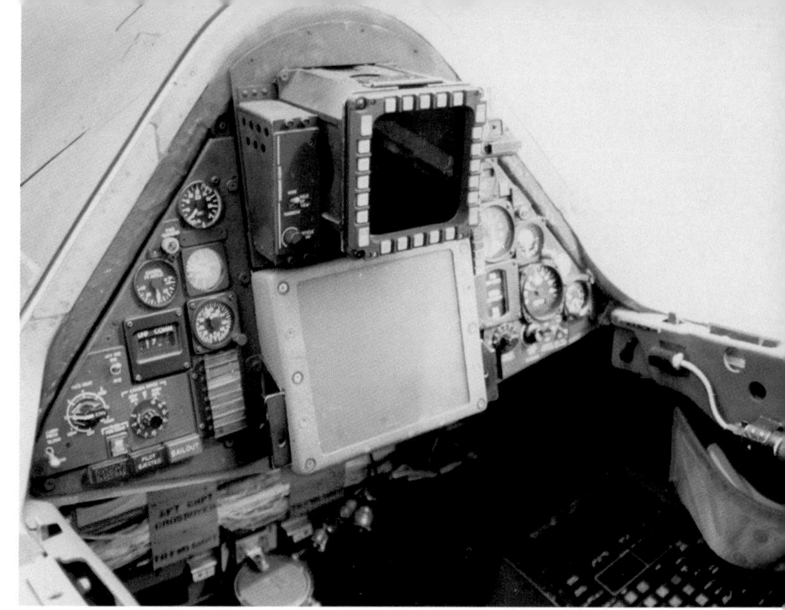

(Above) The Reconnaissance Systems Officer's (RSO's) cockpit had the main panel filled with a large radar screen below the camera system viewing screen (Tony Landis)

(Left) There is nothing remarkable about the pilot's cockpit of an SR-71A. The aircraft used standard instrumentation and, in some respects, was less complex than that of a F-4 Phantom. The pilot's seat has been removed from this SR-71. (Tony Landis)

(Below) Famed Lockheed test pilot (and world's propeller speed record holder) Darrell Greenamyer sits in the cockpit of "Big Tail" Darrell. Air Force Colonels Tom Smith, Tom Pugh and Lockheed Test Pilots Bill Weaver and Daniel Andre were the only five persons to pilot the "Big Tail" SR-71 during the fifteen months that the program flew. (Lockheed via Tony Landis)

Sitting in a puddle of its own fuel, this SR-71A (2015/17964) waits to be pulled outside for display. It was expected that some 400,000 excited spectators would view the aircraft at the annual Offutt Air Force Base open house during 1979. When on the ground, the SR-71 leaked fuel excessively. (Author)

The first of thirty-two SR-71s starts a test flight on 22 December 1964 with test pilot Bob Gilliland at the controls. (Lockheed)

This SR-71 was lost on 25 January 1966 while being flown by Bill Weaver with Jim Zwayer in the rear cockpit. The aircraft, SR-71A (2003/17952), came apart at Mach 3.17 at an altitude of 80,000 feet. Both men got out, but Jim Zwayer did not survive. (Lockheed)

The aft fuselage tooling and assembly area at the "Skunk Works". The aft fuselage on the right was being readied for mating with a completed forward fuselage section. (Lockheed via Author)

"Q" bay sensor location, other types and configurations of sensors had to be designed and qualified.

The first mock-up review of the R-12 by Air Force personnel occurred on 13 and 14 June 1963. Overall reaction from the Air Force team was that they were impressed by what they saw. A final review of the R-12 mock-up was held on 11 December 1963 and by mid-March of 1964 construction of the first six R-12/SR-71s was well on its way.

Operating under a heavy blanket of security, the R-12/SR-71 production continued to operate much the same as its predecessor, the A-12, completely under wraps. The veil of secrecy was finally lifted on 24 July 1964 when President Lyndon B. Johnson made the public announcement of the successful development of major new strategic manned aircraft system which would be employed by the Air Forces Strategic Air Command.

By the end of October of 1964 the first SR-71A, builder's number 2001, Air Force serial 61-7950 was ready for transport from the production facilities in Burbank, California to Lockheed's newest final assembly and flight test center at Air Force Plant 42, Site 2, Palmdale,

Lockheed Test Pilot, Robert J. Gilliland, the first man to fly the SR-71A, poses in front of his favorite aircraft in a first generation SR-71 full pressure flight suit. The box next to his feet was a portable air conditioning unit. (Lockheed)

The number one SR-71A (2001/17950), was being readied for paint at Site 2, the SR-71 Lockheed Flight Test Center, Palmdale, California just a few weeks before its first flight on 22 December 1964. (Lockheed via Author)

California. In the early morning darkness of 29 October 1964, SR-71 number 2001 left for the fifty mile ride to the Palmdale location. As with all the Blackbirds, this was accomplished by two special trailers used to haul the fifteen A-12s and the three YF-12s from Burbank to Area 51. They would be used to carry all thirty-two SR-71s from Burbank to the SR-71 Flight Test Center and final assembly location at Air Force Plant 42, Site 2, Palmdale.

The first flight of SR-71A number 2001 took place on 22 December

This is what is left of the first SR-71A (2001/17950) after an accident at Edwards Air Force Base, California on 10 January 1967. The aircraft was being flown by Lockheed test pilot Art Peterson when it ran off the runway during wet runway braking tests. (Lockheed via Author)

The third SR-71A (2003/17952) is refueled by a KC-135Q tanker over the Mojave Desert of Southern California. This is the SR-71A that disintegrated at Mach 3.17 at over 80,000 feet with Bill Weaver at the controls and Jim Zwayer in the back seat. The loss occurred north of Tucumcary, New Mexico on 25 January 1966. Jim Zwayer did not survive the crash. (Arthor's Collection)

The fourth SR-71A (2004/17953) Blackbird built by Lockheed was lost near Shoshee, California on 18 December 1969 due to a pitch up accident. It was one of four SR-71As and one A-12 lost to this type of accident. At this time the aircraft carried an Outstanding Unit award painted on the fin above the White serial number and a White photographic cross on the engine nacelle just behind the White aircraft side number (953). (USAF via John Andrews)

1964 with Lockheed Test Pilot Robert J. Gilliland at the controls and Jim Eastham flying the F-104 chase plane. This very first flight lasted just over one hour with a top speed in excess of 1,000 mph. Quite an accomplishment for a first fight of any aircraft. Its important to note that on that very same day, some 150 miles to the northeast at the Groom Lake Test Facility, the first flight of the M-21 was also taking place.

On 7 January 1966 the Air Force took delivery of its first SR-71, a SR-71B trainer, number 2007, Air Force serial 61-9756. It was flown from Palmdale to Beale Air Force Base at Marysville, California and accepted by the Air Force. From 7 January 1966 until the very last flight of SR-71 by the Air Force on 6 March 1990, Beale AFB would be home base for the SR-71. Four other locations played host to SR-71s being flown by operating detachments; the 4786th Test Squadron at Edwards AFB, during flight testing from its formation on 1 June 1965; Det 1 of the 9th SRW at Kadena Air Base, Okinawa from March of 1968 until the unit was disbanded during 1989; Det 4 of the 9th SRW at Mildenhall Royal Air Base in the United Kingdom was formed on 31 March 1979; and Det 6 at Air Force Plant 42, Site 2, Palmdale, California, from the beginning of final assembly of the first SR-71 until the end of the program. As it sits today, there are still three SR-71As at Site 2, as well as the last A-12 ever to fly (number 131, Air Force serial 60-06937) which was last flown by Frank Murray on 21 June 1968.

The first mission capable SR-71A to be delivered to the Air Force was accepted and delivered to Beale AFB on 4 April 1966. It was the tenth SR-71A built, number 2009, serial 61-7958. By the end of 1967 all thirty-one SR-71s had been built and delivered with the exception of the thirty-second and final SR-71, the SR-71C trainer, a replacement for the SR71B, number 2008 which was lost on final approach to Beale on 11 January 1968. The SR-71C, number 2000, serial 61-7981, was finally delivered to the Air Force on 14 March 1969. Of the thirty-two SRs built, the first six airframes were relegated to flight test, three for Lockheed and three for Air Force; the 7th, 8th and 32nd SR-71s were configured as SR-71B/C elevated cockpit trainers and were not mission

The fifth SR-71A (2005/17954) on a test flight just before it was lost at Edwards Air Force Base, California. The cause of its accident was wheel/tire failure on take off. (USAF via John Andrews)

Covered with fire fighting foam, the fifth SR-71A built (2005/17954) sits on the Edwards Air Force Base runway after suffering a near fatal wheel disintegration on take off. The pilot, Lieutenant Colonel Bill Skliar was in the middle of a test to determine problems associated with maximum gross weight take offs when a tire and wheel exploded, rupturing the left wing fuel tank causing a massive fire. The cost to repair number 2005 was deemed to be impractical and the SR-71A was written off on 11 April 1969. (Lockheed via Tony Landis)

This view of the SR-71B trainer (2007/17956) was sent to me by Mr. Ben R. Rich when he was Vice President and General Manager of the Lockheed Skunk Works. The addition of the second cockpit had little effect on overall flight characteristics. (Lockheed via Author)

The SR-71B two seat trainer parked on the ramp at Beale Air Force Base, California just after making its one thousandth flight. The second cockpit was raised to allow the rear pilot to see over the aircraft's nose. (Lockheed)

The SR-71C trainer (2000/17981) first took to the air on 14 March 1969 from the Palmdale SR-71 Flight Test Facility at Site 2, with Bob Gilliland at the controls. The last flight was on 11 April 1976. The "Bastard" had only 556.4 hours of flight time and spent the next fifteen years in a hangar at Beale AFB, California before being dismantled and transported via Air Force Reserve C-5A to its final resting place, the Hill AFB Museum, Utah. (Lockheed)

The SR-71B (number 2007/17956) was followed by a Beale AFB assigned T-38A while making the one thousandth flight of the SR-71B. For the special flight, the aircraft carried a large White 1,000 FLT painted on the underside. (Lockheed)

A Lockheed ground crewman communicates with the cockpit crew of NASA's SR-71B, number 831, as they prepare for engine run up at Site 2 prior to making its first flight in NASA markings. It retained its Air Force overall Black color scheme and carried the current style of NASA markings which consist of a White fin band with a Red stylized NASA long on the band. All emergency markings on the aircraft were in Red. (Tony Landis)

A SR-71A (number 2012/17961) inflight over the Folsom Reservoir in northern California. This SR-71A later became a hangar queen at Beale being almost totally stripped of parts by the time the program ended. From its first flight on 9 February 1966 to its last flight on 2 February 1977, 17961 flew a total of 1,601 hours. It is now on display at the Museum of the Cosmos in Hutchingson, Kansas. (USAF via Goodall)

The SR-71A fleet in open storage at Air Force Plant 42, Site 2, Palmdale. The aircraft are listed as being in flyable storage and may be those used if the Air Force follows through on recent plans to bring several Blackbirds back into service. (Lockheed)

The SR-71 overhaul depot at Air Force Plant 42, Site 2, Palmdale, California during the mid-1980s. In addition to the SR-71s undergoing overhaul there are five U-2Rs in the background. Aircraft 2006/17955 is carrying the Skunk Works logo on the fin in Black and White. (Lockheed)

The Outstanding Unit Award was painted on the fin just above the White tail numbers on both fins. The White plus marking on the engine nacelle was used during photo evaluations and was a photographic reference mark. (USAF-via John Andrews)

This Blackbird was named Iche Ban and was one of the more famous SR-71A's to fly. Besides the distinctive White Cobra and Red name on the fin, SR-71A, 2025/17974, also carried twelve mission markings just behind of the RSO's cockpit in White. The aircraft was based at Kadena Air Base Okinawa, Japan and flew reconnaissance missions over North Vietnam. Photographic reconnaissance materials brought back by SR-71s made it possible to construct accurate maps of North Vietnam in support of the B-52 bombing program late in the war. This was the last SR-71 to be lost, when it suffered an engine explosion off the Philippines on 21 April 1989. (USAF via Goodall)

A SR-71A Blackbird (2006/17955) makes a high speed, head on pass at low altitude. (Lockheed via John Andrews)

This SR-71A (2006/17955) was displayed at an Air Force Open House carrying the Lockheed Skunk Works logo, which consisted of a Black and White Skunk insignia, on both vertical fins. (Arthor 's Collection)

capable. That left twenty-five SR-71As (not counting losses) for the operational inventory. At any given time, twenty percent of any aircraft type would be undergoing major phase or modification at the depot or down for scheduled maintenance at the parent unit's location. This left sixteen SR-71As considered fully mission capable, which worked out to two squadrons of nine aircraft, eight SR-71As and a trainer. These squadrons were the 1st SRS and the 99th SRS. As the SR-71A inventory was reduced due to accidents and a reduction in the number of aircraft needed to do the job, the 99th SRS, the "Red Buffalos" was deactivated on 1 April 1971.

Over the thirty years that the Blackbird flew, nineteen were written off; eleven SR-71s were lost; four of the six flight test aircraft, the second SR-71B, number 2008, serial 17957, and six operational SR-71As. One of the three YF-12As that was written off was number 1001/06934 which was dismantled to build the SR-71C trainer. Six of the fifteen A-12s crashed, none to enemy fire. The only person to ever shoot down (figuratively speaking) a Blackbird was then Air Force Chief of Staff, General Larry Welch. In 1989, he shot down the entire fleet in one fell swoop, by ordering its retirement.

A break down of the nineteen Blackbird losses is as follows: four SR-71As, 953, 966, 969 and 970 and one A-12, number 123/926 were lost to pitch up accidents. Three SR-71As, 950, 954 and 977 to wheel and tire failure on takeoff. The second M-21, number 134/941 had a midair collision with a D-21 drone over the Pacific Missile Range off of Point. Mugu, California. A-12 number 129/932 and SR-71A, 953 disintegrated at speeds above Mach 3 and at altitudes above 78,000 feet. A-12 number 125/929 ran out of fuel in-flight and was lost (as was the pilot). A-12 number 126/928 was lost on takeoff due to switched flight controls. A-12 number 133/939 crashed on landing approach at Aera 51 due to a loss of hydraulic control. The second SR-71B number 957 had a total electrical failure and was lost on a landing approach to Beale. The third YF-12A, number 936, suffered a major in-flight fuel fed fire near Edwards AFB, California and crashed, the crew ejected safely. SR-71, number 978 was written off when it ran off the runway in severe cross winds at Kadena Air Base, Okinawa, Japan. The last SR-71, number 974 was written off as a result of a massive engine explosion off the coast of the Island of Luson, in the Philippines. Out of all aircraft losses, only four pilots lost their lives, Ray Torick in the M-21, number 135 at Mach 3.27; Jack Weeks in A-12, number 129 at speeds above Mach 3+, Walt Ray in A-12, number 125 at subsonic speed and Jim Zwayer in SR-71A, 952 at Mach 3.21.

During the buildup of DESERT STORM, the Department of Defense contacted Lockheed and inquired as to how long it would take to pull one of the stored SR-71As from storage at Site 2 and make it fully mission capable. The response from Lockheed was that with, "No administrative overhead, they could hire who they needed and pay what ever price was needed to get the talent, have the highest priority on any and all items needed to complete the job," then Lockheed would be able to provide a SR-71 with crew and spares, mission ready for operations in support of DESERT SHIELD/DESERT STORM within fourteen days from the go ahead. The Department of Defense took several weeks to

The first SR-71B (2007/17956) trainer is readied for its first flight from Site 2 on 18 November 1965. The pilot selected to make the B model's maiden flight was the same man who made the first flight of the first production SR-71A, Lockheed test pilot Bob Gilliland. For this flight, the aircraft carried White photographic calibration crosses on the engine nacelles. The raised second cockpit allowed the second pilot to see over the long nose of the Blackbird. (Lockheed)

A tow vehicle moves the first SR-71B two seat trainer out for its first flight on 18 November 1965. The aircraft was produced when it was found that an operational trainer variant of the Blackbird was necessary to transition service pilots into the Mach 3 aircraft. (Lockheed)

respond to this offer, when they did they asked how long it would take to prepare a second SR-71A for operational missions. Because General Welch had taken great care in taking apart of the SR-71 infrastructure, the second aircraft would take thirty days from go-ahead, due to the need to reassemble sensors and DEF equipment (electronic warfare and defensive equipment). Again it took the DEPARTMENT OF DEFENSE several weeks to respond. When they did the news came as a shock to both Lockheed and the Air Force. The Department of Defense finally came back with the following statement, "Because the Secretary's office had the final say on the deactivation of the SR-71 fleet, to order its reactivation at this time would make the Secretary look bad." Well so much for "National Security".

The SR-71's record for achievement is untouchable by any known aircraft on the drawing board today: 53,490 total flight hours. 17,300 missions flown. Of these, 3,551 were operational reconnaissance missions flown over North Korea, North Vietnam, the Middle East, South Africa, Cuba, Nicaragua, Libya and the Falkland Islands. A total of 11,008 hours flown in support of operational missions. 25,862 in flight refuelings, mostly by KC-135Qs. And an unbelievable 11,675 flight hours at or above Mach 3.0.

Of the twenty-one surviving SR-71s, NASA has three, 956, 971 and 980; three are in what has been referred to as flyable storage at Air Force Plant 42, Site 2 (962, 967 and 968). The balance are on public display at the following museums around the country: 17951 is at the Pima County Air Museum, Tucson, Arizona, 17955, is at the Edwards Flight Test Museum, Edwards AFB, California. 17958, is located at Robins AFB Museum, Warren-Robbins, Georgia. 17959, the only "Big Tail" SR-71 is at the Eglin AFB Armament Museum, Florida. 17960 is resting at the Castle AFB Museum, Merced, California. 17961, is at the Air and Space Museum, Hutchinson, Kansas. 17972, the record holder, is temporarily stored at Dulles Airport near Washington, DC for the Smithsonian Air and Space Museum. 17973, is at Blackbird Park, on the south side of Air Force Plant 42 on Avenue P and 30th in Palmdale, California. The first A-12 is also on display at this location. 17975, is located at the March Air Force Reserve Base, Riverside, California. 17976, the first SR-71 to fly an operational mission, is residing at the Air Force Museum, Wright-Patterson AFB, Dayton, Ohio, along with the only YF-12A (06935) and a D-21B, 17979, is at Lackland AFB, San Antonio, Texas. 17981, the only SR-71C trainer, is displayed at the Hill AFB Museum, Ogden, Utah.

From head on, it is clear that the second cockpit had to be raised to allow the pilot to see over the long nose of the SR-71B. The aircraft was parked on the ramp at Site 2, Palmdale, just prior to delivery to NASA in July of 1991. (Tony Landis)

The number one SR-71B (2007/17956), taxis to the main runway at Air Force Plant 42, Palmdale, California with Bob Gilliland at the controls. The triangle between the cockpits was the Red and White ejection seat warning marking. (Lockheed)

Update:

The FY95 Defense Budget, which both houses of Congress have

For years there was a rumor that a SR-71A (2010/17959) known as "Big Tail", was built with an extended rear fuselage. It wasn't until after the SR-71 program had been terminated that any details of the actual "Big Tail" aircraft actually surfaced. (Lockheed via Tony Landis)

The "Big Tail", SR-71A (number 2010/17959) parked on the ramp at Air Force Plant 42, Site 2, Palmdale, California during 1975. (Lockheed via Tony Landis)

This was the largest single load ever carried inside a cargo aircraft. The Blackbird was one hundred feet long, nineteen feet wide and eleven feet high. It weighed some 21,900 pounds. The A-12 was being delivered to the Minnesota Air National Guard Museum, at Minneapolis/St. Paul International Airport. (Author)

This was the last SR-71A built (2032/17980) and it is still flying today with NASA. The aircraft carries the Red and White NASA band on the fin and a White tail number. All other markings on the aircraft are in Red. The aircraft is used for high speed, high altitude research. (NASA)

This A-12 (130/06933) belongs to the world famous San Diego Aerospace Museum located at Balboa Park, San Diego, California. The restored Blackbird rests on a specially built pylon outside the museum entrance. (Tony Landis)

SR-71B 2007/17956 carried this special marking on the fin in White just after the historic one thousandth flight. Before being turned over to NASA in July of 1991, the sole remaining SR-71B had logged more than 3,760 flight hours. (Lockheed)

passed and sent on to the President for signature, contained 100 million dollars for the reactivation of three SR-71As. These aircraft are to be based at Edwards Air Force Base. Shortly after the first of the year, the SR-71A assigned to NASA, aircraft 2022/17971, will be flown from the NASA Ames/Dryden Flight Test Center at Edwards to Air Force Plant 42, Plamdale, California (a short eight minute flight). 2022/17971, has been in storage at NASA since February of 1990 and has less than five flight hours since its last complete overhaul during 1989.

Once at Plant 42, Site 2, it is estimated that it will take Lockheed technicians four months to upgrade aircraft 2022 to full airworthy, mission ready status. The other two will take an additional eight and nine months respectively from the time Lockheed gets the go-ahead. The prime candidates for the second and third aircraft are 2018/17967 and 2019/17968. Both of these aircraft have the same revisions and updates to the airframe as 2022/17971.

Once the official go-ahead is given, each SR-71A will be stripped down to the airframe, all panels will be removed, fuel tank seals stripped and reinstalled, and some (as yet unidentified) modifications added. Pssible modifications include; real time data link,new mission computers and software and other electronic changes. After this has been completed, all systems will be run-up, new mission ready programs will be loaded into the systems, and a vigorous flight test program will be started, including a number of high speed missions.

Once the three aircraft fleet is back on operational status, money has been funded for one thirty day deployment to a threat area (what-ever area is closest at the time the aircraft are ready). The forward base could be Kadena, Okinawa, Japan (to cover North Korea), Diego Garcia in the Indian Ocean (to cover the Persian Gulf area) or perhaps back to Mildenhall, in the United Kingdom, if the problem area was in Europe. Only time will tell.

Unofficial sources state that depending on the success of the reactiva-

Ground crewmen secure this SR-71A Blackbird, 2009/17958, after a routine training flight in the mid-1970s from Beale Air Force Base, California. Beale was the home for the Blackbird fleet during this time frame. (USAF)

(Above and Below) The second SR-71B, 2008/17957, rests upside down in the middle of a chicken ranch just five miles north of the runway at Beale Air Force Base, California. The SR-71B had suffered total electrical failure over Montana on 11 January 1968 and made it this far before both engines flamed out. The Instructor Pilot, Lieutenant Colonel Robert Sower and the student pilot, Captain David Fruehauf both ejected safely. (Marysville Appeal-Democrate)

The eleventh SR-71A, 2011/17960, taxies in after a flight at Beale AFB, California during the late 1960s. This SR-71A holds the record for the most combat missions flown (342 missions) over Southeast Asia. SR-71A "960" is now on display at the Castle Air Force Base Museum in Merced, California. (USAF via Author)

SR-71A, 2013/17962, takes off from Offutt Air Force Base, Omaha, Nebraska on 9 October 1976. This aircraft is now one of the three SR-71As in storage at Site 2, Palmdale, California. Before the SR-71 program came to an end in January of 1990, 17962 had flown 2,835.7 hours. Its first flight was on 29 April 1966 and its last flight was on 14 February 1990. (Charles B. Mayer)

The White markings on the underside of this SR-71A (2013/17962), were to aid ground tracking stations in monitoring and photographing the aircraft during record setting flights. The light rectangle under the forward cockpit was a Yellow rescue placard. All lettering on this Blackbird was in White. (USAF via Author)

Carrying portable air conditioning units, the flight crew prepares to board a SR-71A on the flight line at Beale Air Force Base. The two crew members are wearing second generation David Clark Company full pressure suits. This SR-71A, (2014/17963) was last flown on 28 October 1976. From its first fight to its last, 17963 flew 1,604.4 hours. It is now on display at the base of the Beale AFB tower. (USAF via Author)

(Left) SR-71A 17963 carried these non-standard 9th SRW markings on the tail, with a full size tail number in Red,during in August of 1990. (Author)

On final approach to Offutt Air Force Base, Omaha, Nebraska, SR-71A (2015/17964) makes a gear down high speed pass down the Offutt runway on 6 July 1979. From its first flight on 11 May 1966 to its last flight to the Strategic Air Museum in Bellerue, Nebraska on 20 March 1990, 17964 flew a total of 3,373.1 hours. (Charles B. Mayer)

The flight crew exits 17964 on the Offutt Air Force Base ramp after a high speed flight from the west coast. The braking parachute door is open and the wheel/brake fans are in place in front of the triple main gear tires to cool down the aircraft's wheels and brakes. The first man out of the Blackbird was the rear seat crewman who quickly opened the faceplate on his helmet. (Charles B. Mayer)

A SR-71A accelerates down the Offutt Air Force Base runway. As the aircraft picks up speed, wing vortices become visible as wisps of vapor. (Charles B. Mayer)

Ground crewmen surround this SR-71A Blackbird on the Offutt Air Force Base ramp as they assist in shutting down the aircraft, its systems, and helping the crew exit the aircraft. A tow bar is in place in front of the nose wheel and will be hooked up once the crew is out and the wheels have cooled down. (Charles B. Mayer)

No one is perfect, are they? This is what happens when you are not paying complete attention to the checklists. This SR-71A reveals what happens when you turn on the aircraft's hydraulic system, forget to install the landing gear locking pins on all wheels, then cycle the gear handle to the up position. The end result is several million dollars in damage to the aircraft and a few lost stripes to the ground crewman. (USAF via Author)

Sitting on the visiting aircraft ramp at Andrews Air Force Base, Maryland, (just outside Washington, DC) with a crew boarding ladder in place, this SR-71A (2018/17967) reveals just how graceful the SR-71A Blackbird appears. In addition to the boarding ladder, the aircraft also has a nose wheel tow bar in place and the drag parachute door is in the open position. (Author's Collection)

(Left) Not every landing is a good one. This SR-71A (17967), decided to take a short cut through the grass at Kadena Air Base, Okinawa, Japan, ending up surrounded by crash trucks in the grass. The damage was minimal and the Blackbird was back in the air in a matter of a week or two. (USAF via Author)

tion of the three SR-71As, it may be possible to reactivate a fourth aircraft (SR-71A 2013/17962). This aircraft has 2,835.9 hours on the airframe. There are a number of officials who feel that the country may need six or seven flyable Blackbirds to be able to cover possible threats. If this comes to pass, then more of the aircraft (there are seven in museums around the country) may be reactivated.

Sporting the new Red low visibility markings introduced on the SR-71 during 1981, this SR-71A (2019/17968) also carried tail art. Most tail art was worn by overseas deployed SR-71As and was not allowed stateside because the brass saw them as unnecessary. This SR-71A first flew on 10 October 1966 and was last flown from Beale Air Force Base to Air Force Plant 42, Site 2, for long term storage just in case the Air Force ever decided it needed the capability of a Mach 3.2 reconnaissance platform. As of its last flight on 12 February 1990, 17968 had flown a total of 2,279.0 hours. (Lockheed via Author)

A SR-71A Blackbird banks as it turns toward final approach to Beale Air Force Base. The aircraft carries Red markings, except for the tail art under the Red fin serial number. The thin White vapor trail behind the Blackbird indicates that the SR-71 is dumping fuel to get down to proper landing weight. (Author's Collection)

This is the only known illustration of the twentieth SR-71 built. This SR-71A (2020/17969) was lost shortly after it completed refueling with a KC-135Q tanker near Bangkok, Thailand. The SR-71A suffered an uncontrollable pitch up on 10 May 1970, due to an improper Center of Gravity (CG) problem. The crew ejected safely but the SR-71A was a write off. (Author's Collection)

A Blackbird prepares to link up with a Beale AFB based KC-135Q tanker. This SR-71A (2018/17967) was last flown on 14 February 1990 and was put into storage at Site 2, Palmdale, California for possible future use by the Air Force. From its first flight on 3 August 1966 to its last flight, 17967 had flown a total of 2,636.8 hours. (Author's Collection)

Deploying its forty-foot drag parachute to slow its speed, this record setting SR-71A (2023/17972) Blackbird lands at Beale Air Force Base, California on 14 May 1981 after capturing the coast to coast speed record. It also holds the world's record time from New York to London, England, one hour and fifty-five minutes and the London to Los Angeles speed run in three hours and forty-seven minutes. When 17972 was retired after its record run on 6 March 1990, it had logged a total of 2,801.1 hours of air time. (Peter B. Lewis)

Family portraits of the Strategic Air Command's finest, the Convair B-58A Hustler (60-2433), the Boeing B-52H (60-0017), a Boeing KC-135 Stratotanker (58-0054), the twenty-first SR-71A (2021/17970) and a T-38 Talon trainer. This SR-71A was lost in a mid-air collision with a KC-135 tanker over El Paso, Texas on 17 June 1970. The tanker made an emergency landing at Briggs Army Air Field near El Paso, Texas and the SR-71A crew, pilot Lieutenant Colonel Buddy Brown and RSO Major Mortimer Jarvis ejected safely. The B-52 is carrying a pair of Hound Dog air launched cruise missiles on its underwing pylons. (USAF via Author)

971 is missing the White buzz number normally carried on the engine nacelle. This SR-71A made its last flight from Beale Air Force Base, California to NASA Dryden at Edwards Air Force Base, California on 19 March 1990. From its first flight on 17 November 1966 to its last, 17971 had flown a total of 3,512.5 hours. It was storaged at NASA/Dryden until 11 January 1995 when it made a ferry flight from Edwards to Air Force Plant 42, Site 2 Palmdale, California for reactivation. (Author)

A SR-71A (2023/17972) taxies down the ramp at Kadena Air Base, Okinawa, Japan during the height of the war in Vietnam. The Blackbirds based at Kadena earned the nickname "Habu", after a very aggressive deadly snake that lived on the island. Some Kadena SR-71As carried tail art depicting a striking snake on the fin under the serial number. (Author's Collection)

A SR-71A lines up on the main runway at Norton Air Force Base, California as it prepares for take off. The Blackbird (17972) carries small Red tail numbers, a Red stencil style national insignia on the fuselage side and Red warning placards under the cockpits. In addition, it carried a Black and White Lockheed Skunk logo on the tail just below the serial number. (Tony Landis)

The tail markings of the record setting SR-71A Blackbird shortly after landing at Dulles Airport just outside Washington, DC. The Air Force Logistics Command logo was carried in a Red stencil style just above the small Red tail numbers and the Black and White Skunk Works logo was just below the tail numbers. This was 61-7972's last flight. (Tony Landis)

With shock cones coming from both engines, this SR-71A (number 17972) conducts its last flyby after making a record one hour six minute coast to coast run from Los Angeles to Washington DC on the morning of 6 March 1990. The flight was not made by members of the Strategic Air Command, but a flight test crew from Site 2, at Palmdale, California. At the time Air Force brass did not want the record set and did everything they could to make it next to impossible to pull off. It was also the first and only time a SR-71A wore the Air Force Logistic Command badge on its tail. (Tony Landis)

There are three camera windows visible on the underside of this SR-71A (2022/17971). There are two under the fuselage, one under the U.S. Air Force and one under the national insignia. Visible under the nose is the third window for the Optical Bar Camera (OBC) system. (USAF via Author)

A SR-71A (2026/17975) takes off on a very hot and humid day at Beale Air Force Base. The aircraft's main landing gear doors are beginning to close and it is streaming wingtip and bobtail vapor trails as it climbs out to the south. From its first flight on 13 April 1967 to its last on 28 February 1990, when it was ferried from Beale Air Force Base, California to its final resting place at March Air Force Reserve Base near Riverside, California, 17975 had logged a total of 2,854.0 hours of flight time. (Author)

The twenty-fourth SR-71 carried an interim low visibility paint scheme. The national insignia is in Flat Red and a Red USAF appears just above the Flat Red tail numbers. This SR-71A (2024/17973) was retired after its last flight on 21 July 1987, when a young SR-71 pilot almost broke the airframe in half by pulling too many "Gs". Rather than replace all the bolts at the 715 splice, the SR-71A was flown at speed from Mildenhall RAF base in the United Kingdom to Palmdale where is was retired. First flown on 8 February 1967, 17973 logged a total of 1,729.6 flight hours before its untimely retirement. It is now a companion to the very first A-12, number 121, at the Blackbird Park in Palmdale, California. (Author)

Flying with the test group out of Site 2, Palmdale, California, this SR-71A (17974) climbs out to the west trailing vapor trails as it flies over the Sierra Highway that parallels the Southern Pacific railroad tracks. This SR-71A was lost on 21 April 1989 off the coast of the Island of Luzon in the Philippines due to a catastrophic engine failure. The crew ejected successfully, made it to shore and was rescued by one of the island's former cannibal tribes. (Lockheed)

Being chased by two Northrop T-38A Talons, one from the flight test center and one from NASA, this SR-71A (17973) can be seen venting fuel from the fuel dump drain located in the bobtail as it flies past Site 3 at Palmdale. The aircraft carries the Lockheed Skunk insignia on the fin just below the White tail numbers. The flight test center Talon carries a Black SR-71 marking on its fin above the serial number. Both Talons are in the same overall color scheme, overall White with Blue trim. (Lockheed)

These aircraft are on static display at Blackbird Park, located at the corner of Avenue P and 30th street in Palmdale, California. The SR-71A carries the low-vis Red markings with no national insignia and the A-12 carries the White markings with full color national insignia. (Tony Landis)

This was the first SR-71A to fly an operational reconnaissance mission out of Kadena Air Base, Okinawa, Japan, flown by then Major Jerry O'Malley with Major Ed Payne as his RSO. It flew its first operational mission on 26 March 1968 over North Vietnam. From its first flight on 16 May 1967, until its retirement to the Air Force Museum on 27 March 1990, "976" had flown a total of 2,985.7 hours. (Author's Collection)

This is what was left of "Rapid Rabbit" (2029/17919) after a landing accident at Kadena Air Base, Okinawa, Japan on 20 July 1972. The pilot, Major Dennis Bush and RSO, Captain James Fagg came out of the crash okay. Most of the damage was caused in the attempt to destroy "978" by fire. As it turns out titanium does burn very well. What was left of the airframe was buried at Kadena. (Author's Collection)

A SR-71A Blackbird (17976) is watched over by a crash truck as it sits in the turf after running off the taxiway at Beale Air Force Base, California. It is believed that the accident was caused by excessive speed when the aircraft attempted to make the turn off the runway and onto the taxiway. The damage appears to be minor in nature. (USAF via Author)

After completing another mission, this SR-71A Blackbird (17979) taxies north to its hangar at Beale Air Force Base, California. The drag chute doors are open and will remain so until the repacked chute is reloaded into the compartment. The SR-71A had a large landing light mounted on the nose wheel strut. (Charles B. Mayer)

This is what happens when you have a wheel and tire failure on take off. Couple that with running over a six foot drainage ditch and the result is the total loss of the twenty-eighth SR-71A (2028/17977). This accident happened on 10 October 1968 on the north end of the Beale Air Force Base runway. The RSO decided to eject, while the pilot, Major Gabrial Kardong stayed with the aircraft. When the SR stopped moving, Major Kardong opened the canopy and stepped out, without a scratch. Once he was clear, the aircraft was covered with fire fighting foam by the crash crew. (Marysville Appeal-Democrat)

The crash crew and base security was quick to respond to Major Gabrial Kardong's accident, covering the damaged Blackbird with fire smothering foam. The landing gear was totally torn from the aircraft after one wheel/tire failed on take off from Beale Air Force Base on 10 October 1968, causing the aircraft to leave the runway and impact a six foot drainage ditch. Both crewmen escaped from the crash and Major Kardong was completely uninjured. (Marysville Appeal-Democrat)

(Left) A SR-71A (2031/17988) conducts a fly by at Greenham Common, England during the annual air show in the Summer of 1983. This SR-71A spent most of its flying career with Det 4 at Mildenhall RAF base in the United Kingdom. When it was turned over to NASA in February of 1990, it had flown 2,255.6 hours with the Air Force. (Author's Collection)

A SR-71A rolls past "HABU Hill" located just off base at Kadena Air Base, Okinawa. The last flight for SR-71A (2030/17979) was on 6 March 1990 when it flew to Kelly Air Force Base, Texas for permanent display at the Air Force Basic Training Center, Lackland Air Force Base, San Antonio, Texas. From its first flight on 10 August 1967 to its last flight, 17979 logged a total of 3,321.7 flight hours. (Author's Collection)

The world famous "Rapid Rabbit," a high time combat veteran SR-71A (2029/17978) flies over the snow-covered peak of Mount Shasta in northern California. The aircraft carried the world famous Playboy bunny logo on the fin in White. (Lockheed via Author)

"Rapid Rabbit" shares the ramp with two KC-135 tankers while it awaits repairs at Osan Air Force Base, Korea. On its last mission, the "Rabbit" was directed to return to Okinawa, even though there were typhoon conditions at the base. The aircraft made two landing attempts. On the second try, it left the runway and was severely damaged. The "Rabbit" ended its flying carrier and became a parts supply airframe for other Kadena based SR-71s. (David Bolsted)

Ground crews bring up an aircraft powercart to "Rapid Rabbit" which was making an unscheduled visit to Osan Air Base, Korea. The "Rabbit" was secured from view by the many on-lookers by a pair of Kadena based KC-135s. (David Bolsted)

A SR-71 (2031/ 17980) flies over the British country side with a RAF Jaguar strike fighter. The Blackbird was the last SR-71A built and made its first flight on 25 September 1967. It was transferred to NASA on 15 February 1990 where it remains the world's only SR-71A still flying today. (Author's Collection)

The last flying SR-71A (2031/17980) retains its USAF overall Black color scheme with a White tail band, Red NASA logo (known as the NASA worm), White, NASA assigned tail number 844 and Red warning placards under the cockpit area. The aircraft operated out of NASA Ames/Dryden Flight Research at Edwards Air Force Base, California. (NASA)

SR-71A (17976) carried a variation of the Black and White Lockheed Skunk logo on its tail just under the White tail number. There are three camera windows visible along the fuselage undersurface just ahead of the engine nacelle. (USAF via Author)

This SR-71A (17976) is unusual in that it carried a full color 9th Strategic Reconnaissance Wing badge on the fin under the White tail numbers. (USAF via Author)

This was the only SR-71C (2000/17981) ever built. Made up of the rear fuselage of the first YF-12A (1001/06934) and an engineering mockup forward fuselage, the SR-71C was always referred to at the "Bastard." The aircraft made its first flight on 14 March 1969 from the Palmdale SR-71 Flight Test Facility at Site 2, with Bob Gilliland at the controls. The last flight was on 11 April 1976. The "Bastard" spent the next fifteen years in a hangar at Beale Air Force Base, before being dismantled and transported via Air Force Reserve C-SA to its final resting place, the Hill Air Force Base Museum, Ogden, Utah. (Brian C. Rogers)

The SR-71B (2007/17956) painted in new style NASA markings. The tail band is White with the Red NASA logo (also known as the NASA "Worm") with thin Red bands at the top and bottom of the tail band. The tail number 831 is in White and all other markings (rescue markings and warning placards) are in Flat Red. (Tony Landis)

NASA's SR-71B flies over the Edwards Air Force Base complex. Built as a two seat pilot conversion/transition trainer, the SR-71B was never configured for active reconnaissance missions. In NASA service the aircraft has been fitted with a number of test instruments, but its primary mission was still training of NASA pilots scheduled to fly the other SR-71s in the inventory. (NASA via Carla Thomas)

Three training variants of the SR-71 have been built, two SR-71Bs and one SR-71C, of these only 831 is still active, training pilots for NASA on the SR-71's flight characteristics. The elevated rear cockpit is necessary to allow the rear cockpit pilot to see over the nose. (Tony Landis)

The open hatch behind the second cockpit is the refueling port hatch. It is outlined in Red and White to assist the KC-135Q boom operator in locating the hatch. The Red outlined area on the fuselage is a "No Step" area. (NASA via Carla Thomas)

The NASA SR-71B takes off trailing shock cones behind the engines. Besides the elevated rear cockpit, another identifying feature of the SR-71B are the two ventral fins mounted under the engine nacelles to aid in lateral stability. These were added when it became apparent that the addition of the second cockpit adversely affected stability. (NASA via Carla Thomas)

The NASA SR-71B flies high over the California Sierra mountains near Edwards Air Force Base on a training mission out of the Edwards complex. The aircraft is operated by the National Aeronautics and Space Administration as part of its high speed flight research program headquartered at the Ames/Dryden Flight Research Center (Edwards AFB). Before being turned over to NASA, this SR-71B had logged some 3,760 flight hours with the USAF. (NASA via Carla Thomas)

The SR-71B's new National Aeronautics and Space Administration tail markings include the new NASA logo, a White 831 tail number and the former Air Force serial (17956) in Flat Red. All stenciling on the aircraft is in Flat Red. (Tony Landis)

The NASA SR-71B deploys its Red forty foot drag chute after landing on its first mission after a two year lay-off. (Tony Landis)

Big Tail (SR-71A/BT 2010/17959)

The concept of the "Big Tail" was born out of an Air Force study as to ways to enhance the then current fleet of Blackbirds. Numerous studies were looked at to add additional sensors and capabilities to the aircraft without re-manufacturing the entire fleet of SR-71As. One method studied was the addition of belly pods for ECM and Signet. This was considered for a time, but was dropped in favor of an eight foot extension to the existing bobtail. The new "Big Tail" assembly had to be articulated to clear the runways on take off and landing. Once in the air, the tail could be used to help trim the SR-71A.

The assembly had a total up/down movement of eight and a half degrees on either side of center. On landing approach, the tail was moved to the full up position. As the wheels touched down and prior to deployment of the forty foot drag parachute, the tail was moved to the full down position so as not to interfere with the deployment of the drag chute.

Housed inside the movable "Big Tail" was various combinations of sensors and other reconnaissance gear. One combination was ASLAR or radar mapping in the nose with a Optical Bar Camera (OBC) unit in the "Big Tail." Another consideration was to install a real time satellite data link antenna in the tail to allow for real time transmission of reconnaissance results from the Blackbird back to Washington, or to field commanders, or intelligence centers as needed.

The first flight of of the "Big Tail" configuration was on 3 December 1974 and the last flight on 29 October 1976. The "Big Tail" delivered what Lockheed had promised; however, by now the war in Southeast Asia had ended and the Air Force was no longer interested in a production program for the aircraft. With that decision, "Big Tail", with only 866.1 hours on the airframe was stricken from the inventory and placed in outside storage at Air Force Plant 42, Site 2, Palmdale, California. Later the aircraft was dismantled and transported by road to the Armament Museum at Eglin Air Force Base, Florida during the Fall of 1991.

(Right) Who said dummies could not be trained to fly in the Blackbird? This dummies name was "Sierra Sam" and he was used to provided proper weight and balance to "Big Tail" on some of its test and evaluation flights. (Lockheed via Tony Landis)

Bob Murphy, Director for Manufacturing for Lockheed California (Left), Air Force Colonel Tom Jones (center) and Mr. Ben R. Rich, Vice-President and General Manager of the Lockheed Skunk Works (right) look over some of the internal duct work needed for the movable tail assembly on "Big Tail" during the aircraft's construction. (Lockheed via Author)

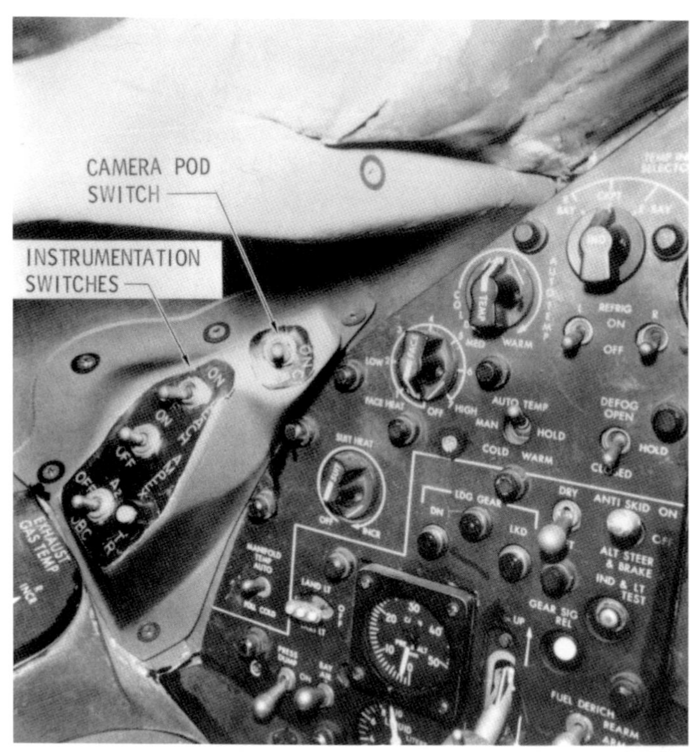

The front cockpit of "Big Tail" had several modifications added to it to control the movable tail section. The mission specific modifications that were required for the flight test are annotated. (Lockheed via Tony Landis)

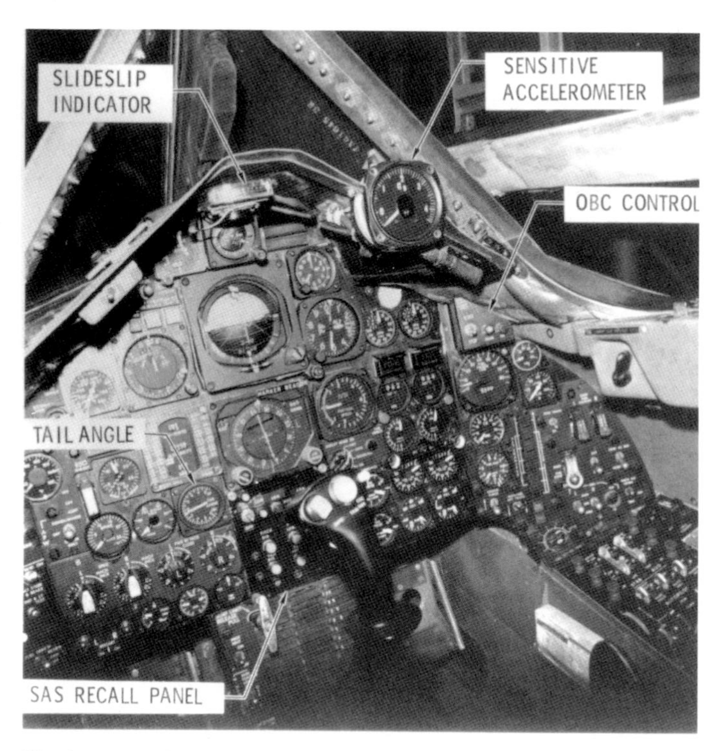

The forward left side instrument panel of the SR-71/BT with the "Big Tail" camera control panel. This panel was used during the operation of the Optical Bar Camera carried in the movable "Big Tail" assembly. The Optical Bar Camera was a thirty inch focal length panoramic scanning camera designed to take photos of a 180 degree sweep below the aircraft. This same camera had been carried in the nose of some SR-71As. (Lockheed via Tony Landis)

The "Big Tail" SR-71 with the movable tail in the full 8.5 degrees up position. This would be the position of the tail at the time of landing. Just after the wheels touched down, the tail would move to the full down position to avoid blocking the operation of the drag chute. (Lockheed via Tony Landis)

A KC-135Q refuels a SR-71A/BT "Big Tail" over the Mojave Desert. The aircraft carried the standard Blackbird colors of overall Black with White lettering. The tail is in the down position, which would be the normal position for a photographic run. In the air, the tail could be used to help trim the SR-71A/BT. (Lockheed via Tony Landis)

The SR-71A/BT parked on the ramp with the "Big Tail" in the full up position. The panoramic window for the Optical Bar Camera (OBC) system is visible on the underside of the movable tail just to the rear of the wing trailing edge. The first flight of the "Big Tail" configuration was on 3 December 1974. Although the aircraft was fully mission capable, the end of the war in Vietnam caused the Air Force to lose interest in this modification and the program was cancelled. (Lockheed via Tony Landis)

The SR-71A/BT "Big Tail" pops its drag chute on the Palmdale main runway after returning from one of its first flights, During the early test flights, the movable "Big Tail" had photographic reference lines painted in White down each side of the tail. Just as the drag chute is deployed, the "Big Tail" drops down to the full 8.5 degrees of travel and stays in the full down position until raised by the pilot. (Lockheed via Tony Landis)

To keep from being cooked on the Lockheed Palmdale, California flight line in 118 degree F heat, movable sunshades were used to cover the Blackbirds. Lockheed technicians are preparing the SR-71A/BT "Big Tail" (background) and another SR-71A for test flights. (Lockheed via Author)

The SR-71A/BT takes on fuel from a SAC KC-135Q tanker during one of the early test flights. The large panoramic window for the Optical Bar Camera (OBC) system is visible under the tail. (Lockheed via Tony Landis)

Pratt & Whitney J-58

One of the critical technical problem in creating a Mach 3 power plant was the development of the new materials needed to withstand the stress of the high inlet operating temperatures. A Mach 0.8 engine operating between 36,000 and 82,000 feet altitude had an inlet temperature of 0 degrees F, but airflow into a Mach 2 engine was raised to approximately 230 degrees F. For Mach 3 flight, the air coming through the inlet to the face of the power plant was at 825 degrees F. Operation of the engines compressor raised the airflow temperature to more than 1,200 degrees F. In addition to the materials problem, there was the basic task of developing an engine with sufficient thrust to push a 150,000 pound aircraft at three times the speed of sound. Pratt & Whitney's J-75 engine was capable of Mach 2, but it was too heavy for satisfactory performance in sustained supersonic flight. A higher specific thrust and lower specific fuel consumption had to be built into any new engine to fulfill the range and speed requirements of a future strategic reconnaissance aircraft.

The birth of the J-58 can be traced back to the Pratt & Whitney J-91 (JT-9) power plant for the cancelled XB-70 program. In the Fall of 1954, the Power Plant Laboratory at Wright Field launched several engine programs in anticipation of the bomber requirements for power plants with airflow between 380 and 400 pounds per second. Two propulsion units were especially promising, the J-89 turbojet, developed by the Allison Division of General Motors, providing a supersonic dash capability with subsonic cruise potential and the all-supersonic J-91 from Pratt & Whitney. The J-89 provided an airflow rate of 380 pounds per second and a 10:1 pressure ratio, while the J-91 handled a 400 pound per second airflow and had a 7:1 pressure ratio.

By late 1955 the number of engines under consideration grew from two to six. Wright Aeronautical had come up with a proposal for an improved J-67 which the company called the TJ32C4. Pratt & Whitney offered the J-91, once envisioned for the Aircraft Nuclear Propulsion (ANP) program, as well as an improved J-75. The other engines now in the running were proposed by General Electric, the TF-31 (X-84) turbofan engine and at least two advanced versions of the J-79. One, which the company designated the X-207, raised the thrust from approximately 15,000 to 18,000 pounds. While the second, the X-275 had some 20,700 pounds of thrust. This GE design (X-275) was specifically to meet the early requirements stated for the future strategic bomber. By early 1956, the only three power plants on the list were still actively supported by the Air Force, the Allison J-58, the Pratt & Whitney J-91 and the GE X-275.

The J-89 and J-91 engines gradually changed into power plants specifically tailored to the needs of the advanced bomber. The giant J-91 was scaled down and transformed into a Mach 3 engine for the Navy and became the J-58 turbojet. The GE X-275 improvement of the basic J-79 ultimately became the X-279, an engine proposal which, in time, became the J-93, the power plant chosen for the new strategic bomber, the North American XB-70 and the ill fated F-108.

The J-58 program began in earnest as a Navy project during late 1956. It was to be an afterburning turbojet rated at 26,000 pounds of thrust and was to power an advanced variant of the North American A3J-l, later to be called the RA-5C Vigilante.

In 1957, the Navy project was started at the Hartford, Connecticut facilities of Pratt & Whitney under the designation J-58-P2. The number of people working on the program during the development and demonstration phase consisted of twenty-seven project engineers. The total number of support personnel never exceeded 2,500.

The Air Force, not wanting to let its investment get too far from reach, continued to monitor the Navy's progress on the J-58-P2, with the concern expressed about the power plant for the new strategic bomber. It was duly noted to the commander of the Air Research and Development Center in September of 1957, that the Air Force had already invested twenty-five million dollars and three years of work in the J-91 (J-58), resulting in a Mach 3 engine with an accumulated test total of twenty hours of running time and a two or three year development advantage over the J-93.

On 6 November 1957, the J-93 was selected as the only power plant for the new manned bomber and development was to continue unabated. Support for the J-91 was to end since the budget permitted only one Mach 3 turbojet project in fiscal year 1958.

In lieu of a second development effort, the Air Force would monitor Pratt & Whitney's J-58 Navy program with special attention to a modified design to be almost interchangeable with the J-93.

In developing the basic J-58-P2, the state of the art in power plant materials had to take a giant step forward. Materials that were once used

A full scale mock-up of the P-4 variant of the basic J-58 engine rests on an engine stand at the Pratt & Whitney facility in East Hartford, Connecticut, on 24 July 1961. This mock-up was used to determine engine size and weight. (Pratt & Whitney)

to forge turbine blades were now under evaluation for use in the basic structure of the J-58-P2. A material used in the manufacture of watch springs was identified as having the characteristics needed in an engine where flight temperatures would reach 3,200 degrees F. Hamilton watch company provided Pratt & Whitney with a material called Wasaloly. The trick now was to learn how to work a material that started its life as a turbine blade casting/forging and treat it like sheet metal. Many hours of trial and error were consumed in the creation of the material finally chosen for most of the components in the J-58, Astralloy. The testimonial of the strength of this material can be seen in the afterburner section of the current J-58. The entire aft section of the power plant is a mere .030 inches thick.

Once Pratt & Whitney had learned to form the turbine blade material into a sheet metal, they had to overcome the problems of welding this material successfully. Along with the casing structure, all of the internal components i.e., the shafts, disks, even the lubrication pumps had to be fabricated from materials made from the temperature resistant turbine blade type metals and nothing that had ever been developed for any other Pratt & Whitney engine could be used in the J-58.

The original J-58-P2 was developed as a non-afterburning engine. The follow-on engine was designated the J-58-P4. The P4 had the distinction of using blown air taken off the turbine bleed to operate the flight controls of the host aircraft. Other than a full scale mock-up, the P4 version never flew.

As originally conceived, the J-58 fuel was JP-5 but it was later changed to JP-7. The newly developed fuel withstood incredible heat but provided absolutely no lubrication. To overcome this problem, a small amount of fluorocarbon finally had to be added to insure that the engine pumps and servos worked. Because of its operating environment, the fuel was the only option available at the time for use in the engine as a hydraulic fluid to activate the bleeds, afterburner nozzle, etc. The system had no way of cooling the fuel down once it passed through the power plants hydraulic system. It was pumped directly into the engine and consumed.

JP-7, in the past, has been identified in numerous articles as having its own oxidizers, of being a boron type fuel. The truth of the matter is JP-7 is as close to the true definition of JP-1 as any fuel could get. With the exception of the fluorocarbon mixture used for the lubrication of the J-58 controls, JP-7 is very pure kerosene.

The extremely harsh environment presented a severe cooling problem. The primary items to cool were the pilot and the complex electronics and recon equipment. The result was little or no heat sink in the fuel to cool the rest of the airframe or the power plant. The net result is that the electronics used on the J-58 is a fuel cooled solenoid and a trim motor buried deep inside the engine fuel control system. Not wanting to add any item that might fail at high temperatures, it was decided to use a chemical ignition system using tetraethylborane, more commonly referred to as TEB. TEB is used for starting both the main engine and the afterburner. TEB is injected into the ignitor portion of the J-58 using gaseous nitrogen and ignites on contact with any hydrocarbon based fuel (or anything else for that matter).

The use of a chemical ignitor versus an electronic system had its origins in the 1953/1954 time frame. During that period, the Navy was having blow out problems with the J-65 jet engine while the aircraft was airborne. It was not possible to consistently relight the engine with an electrical ignitor. The pilot would try to relight once, maybe twice, then he would eject from the stricken jet. In an attempt to solve this problem, a chemical ignition system using TEB was successfully developed for the Navy. It was flight tested but never adopted.

As the J-58 matured from its beginnings as the J-91 to the J-5 8-P2, its overall appearance began to change. It was obvious by the early part of 1958, that the J-58 would not fit any of the proposed aircraft that the Navy had on the drawing board. There was the problem of flight testing major components when you had no aircraft on which to mount the J-58.

The large White pipe coming out of the center of this J-58 engine mock-up was the bleed air feed pipe. Bleed air was to be used to control the pitch and yaw for an advanced version of the North American (Rockwell) RA-5C Vigilante reconnaissance aircraft. (Pratt & Whitney)

A Pratt & Whitney engineer makes a minor adjustment to a J-58 model K engine on an overhead engine hoist at the Pratt & Whitney Hartford facility during the mid-1960s. These hoists were used to move engines from one location to another around the plant. There were many new materials used in the J-58 and, along with the casing structure, all of the internal components i.e., the shafts, disks, even the lubrication pumps had to be fabricated from materials made from the temperature resistant turbine blade type metals. (Pratt & Whitney)

The YJ-58 service test version of the J-58 engine had 24 ct. Gold plated engine parts. The YJ-58 was used to power the Lockheed A-12 and early YF-12As. Non gold plated engines are used on all SR-71 Blackbirds and are referred to as modelK engines. (Pratt & Whitney via John Andrews)

The answer for Pratt & Whitney was to flight test various major subsystems, such as the exhaust ejectors on modified J-57 jet engines.

If overcoming all the obstacles encountered in developing materials to survive the rugged environment that the J-58 would operate in was not enough, it was necessary to develop a bridge from the experimental/design phase to the development and testing phases. At the time that the engine was being designed, there were no test stands or facilities capable of simulating the operating conditions and extreme temperatures encountered during Mach 3 flight. Pratt & Whitney again was forced to shoot from the hip. If one was not available, then the only alternative was to build one yourself. The heated inlet test stand built by Pratt & Whitney consisted of a J-75 slave engine. The exhaust of the engine was used to approximate the extremes of heat found at high speeds. The stand was able to control the environment from Mach 3.8 at 78,000 feet to Mach 3.5 at 120,000 feet. 1958 was the beginning of the transition from a Navy engine to a power plant for the CIA/USAF OXCART program.

Pratt & Whitney started to work with two major aerospace firms in the design and fabrication of an aircraft designed to fly at Mach 4 at 100,000 feet. The two companies involved in the project were Lockheed and General Dynamics. By this time, the J-58 in all of its forms had accumulated 700 hours of full scale testing and was considered as the prime power plant for these studies. Most of the Pratt & Whitney Hartford employees who had spent the last three to four years

A standard production J-58 engine rests on an engine stand at the Lockheed SR-71 Flight Test Facility at Air Force Plant 42, Slte 2, Palmdale, California. This was the standard engine used on all variants of the SR-71. (Lockheed)

The exhaust of a J-58 jet engine. Many hours of trial and error were consumed in the creation of the material finally chosen for most of the components in the J-58, Astralloy. The strength of this material can be seen in the afterburner section of the current J-58. The entire aft section of the power plant is a mere .030 inches thick. (Author's Collection)

working on the Navy project were informed that the Navy was putting the program on the back burner until a suitable airframe could be developed that would take full advantage of the awesome power of the J-58. They were also led to believe that General Dynamics was interested in the J-58 for use in an advanced version of the B-58 Hustler. This gave legitimacy to the frequent visits by General Dynamics engineers to the Hartford facilities.

During this transition period only a handful of Pratt & Whitney personnel knew what the eventual use for the J-58 was. The entire time the J-58 was a Navy project, the program was open and security was not the word for the day. It was just a Navy program to build an engine for some yet to be designed aircraft. Well, the tune changed. Now that the program was keyed to a CIA/USAF mission, the covers were pulled over the entire program. An example of the shift in mood was best described by an engineer who started on the J-58 program in 1956. He left Hartford for the West Palm Beach facility in mid-1957 to work on commercial engines. In mid-1959, his program was completed at West Palm Beach and he was reassigned back to Hartford. When he returned he asked a senior manager about the status of the J-58, which he thought was a defunct program. He was promptly instructed by the manager and shortly afterward by security not to discuss, speculate, or ask questions about the "defunct" program.

On 29 August 1959, the Lockheed A-12 design was declared the winner and the General Dynamics design, known as the Kingfish, the loser.

The key to the entire Blackbird program can be traced to the hand in hand working relationship developed between Lockheed and Pratt & Whitney. This open working relationship resulted in the ability of both companies to make the advances in the state-of-the-art as needed to achieve the best possible engine/airframe combinations.

With the A-12 approaching production roll out, the incredible iron horse of an engine, the J-58, was nearing the end of the preflight rating tests. This was July of 1962, three years and four months after the go-ahead. The model qualification test was completed in September of 1963. It must be noted that the first A-12s were not powered by J-58s but by two afterburning Pratt & Whitney J-75s. This allowed Lockheed to evaluate the A-12 at subsonic and low Mach numbers while working out problems associated with system integrations. This also gave Pratt & Whitney a chance to work out all the bugs and to bring the J-58 into full production.

The first flight of a J-58 powered A-12 was on 5 October 1962. The combination was a proven J-75 in the starboard nacelle and the J-58 in the port nacelle. The first pure J-58 powered flight was made on 15 January 1963, in aircraft number 121. It was not until 20 July 1963 and 66 lights later that the first Mach 3 flight was made by Lou Schalk.

Once the J-58 was in an airframe designed to operate in the arena that it was created for, other problems began to appear. When heated, the J-58 grows, as does the airframe. The Blackbird grows several inches when hot. The J-58, on the other hand, grows only about 3/4 of an inch. This had been identified during the initial test phase of the engine, but as with all controlled testing, the human factor remained an unknown.

The engine bay access doors are all open as Lockheed technicians prepare to change the J-58 engine on a SR-71A. An engine change operation on a Blackbird was an all day event, even with highly trained personnel, operating under ideal conditions, it would take at least eight hours. (Tony Landis Collection)

Technical Sergeant Lyons uses a flashlight to inspect the afterburner section of a J-58 engine installed in a SR-71 Blackbird. The overall thrust at sea level of a J-58 engine is 32,500 pounds. (Lockheed)

As mentioned earlier, fuel is used to cool the engine. At the end of a typical mission, fuel is low and the amount available for cooling is critical. Two conflicting conditions can destroy the power plant and must be controlled by the pilot. If he descends too slowly, he will run out of fuel to cool the engine. If, on the other hand, he descends too rapidly, the outer casing of the engine will shrink faster than the turbine blades, causing the engine to bind. If that happens, you have a real problem on your hands.

The J-58 was manufactured, over the entire life of production run, at the Hartford, Connecticut plant. Production deliveries began in 1962 and continued through 1969. During this time approximately 150 engines were manufactured with half that number still around today. It is interesting to note that the last major improvement to the current J-58 was made in 1967. That is almost twenty-five years ago. It remains the only Mach 3 rated engine in our inventory.

Cameras

Very little has been made available about the SR-71A reconnaissance sensors. One of the main systems is the LOROP camera made by Itek. This is a sixty-six inch focal length reconnaissance camera, ideal for photographic mapping of large areas. Resolution of this type of system is thirty inches at sixty miles. Cameras are mounted in five major bays within the fuselage and nose. In addition to the camera systems, the SR-71 is also equipped with infrared and digital systems along with various electronic systems,

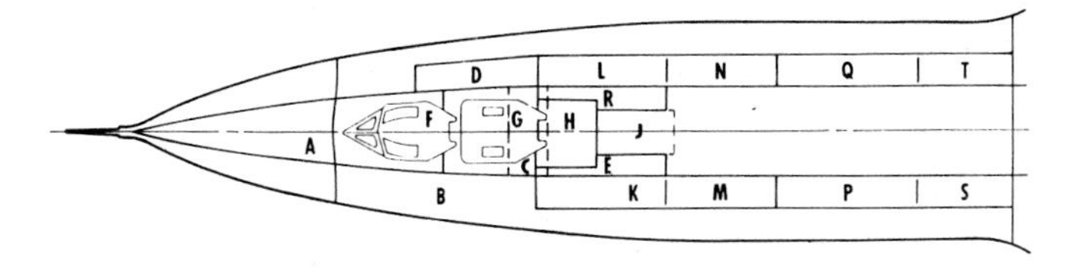

BAY IDENTIFICATION

A	NOSE	M	RIGHT EMR BAY
B	LEFT CHINE	N	RADAR RECORDER BAY
C	TERRAIN CAMERA BAY (C-BAY)	P	LEFT TEOC BAY
D	RIGHT CHINE BAY (FS 305-389)	Q	RIGHT TEOC BAY
E	ELECTRICAL EQUIPMENT BAY (E-BAY)	R	RADIO EQUIPMENT BAY (R-BAY)
F	FORWARD COCKPIT	S	LEFT OOC BAY
G	AFT COCKPIT	T	RIGHT OOC BAY
H	AIR CONDITIONING BAY (AC-BAY)	U	MAIN WHEEL WELL
J	NOSE WHEEL WELL	V	MISCELLANEOUS - FUSELAGE
K	LEFT EMR BAY	W	MISCELLANEOUS - NACELLES
L	RIGHT EMR BAY		

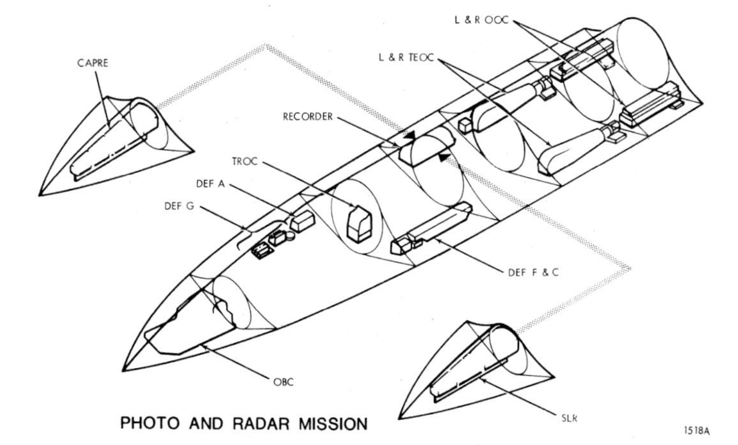

PHOTO AND RADAR MISSION

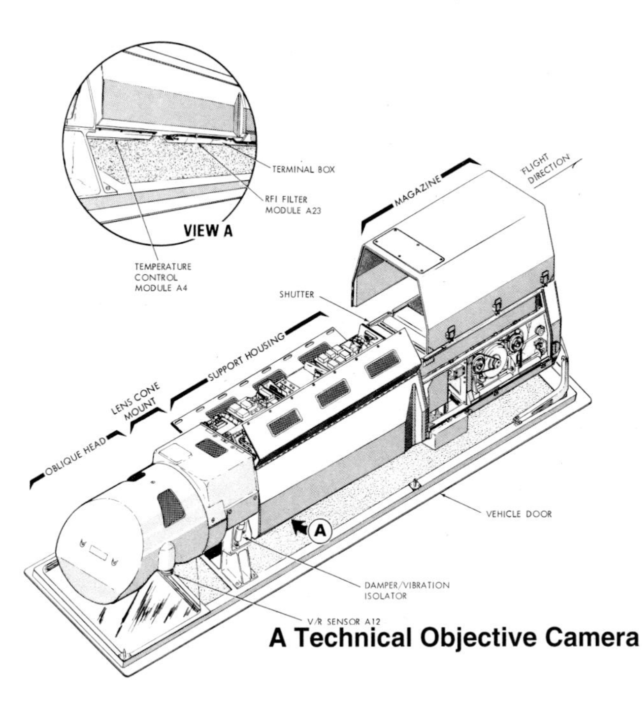

A Technical Objective Camera

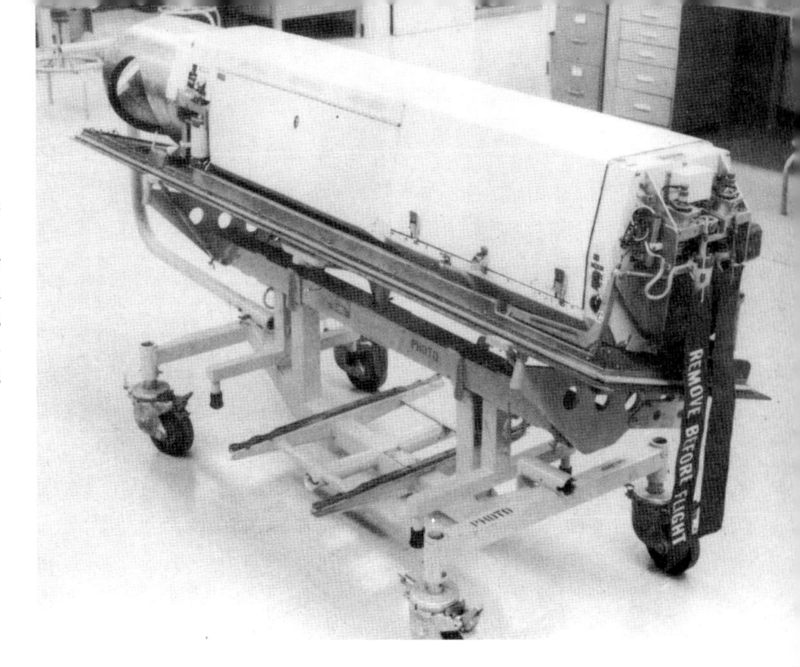

The Technical Objective Camera (TEOC) was one of the primary camera systems and was normally carried in rear camera bays on the SR-71. (USAF)

This is the thirty inch focal length Optical Bar Camera (OBC) that was used in the nose of the SR-71A as a panoramic camera. It was also installed in the movable tail on the ST-71A/BT "Big Tail." (USAF)

Blackbird Details

This is the nose wheel of an A-12 Blackbird. which was the same on all other Blackbirds. A-12 nose wheel assemblies were either Gloss White or Natural Metal. (Author)

The nose wheel assembly of the SR-71 has two lights mounted on the nose wheel strut. The SR-71 wheel assembly was usually painted Black. The housing next to the small light is the nose wheel steering system. (Author)

The SR-71 and A-12 used the same three wheeled main landing gear configuration. This main wheel assembly is from an A-12. The wheel was a forged Titanium hub that was painted either Gloss Insignia Red or Gloss Green. (Author)

This is the pilot's cockpit of an operational SR-71 Blackbird. The cockpit interior color is Medium Gray with the main instrument panel being Flat Black. The two large instruments in the center are the compass and artificial horizon. (Tony Landis)

This is the right side panel in the pilot's cockpit of an operational SR-71. The panel contains the auto pilot controls and circuit breaker panels. The panel color is Medium Gray with Black boxes. Some of the circuit breaker panels are in Red. (Tony Landis)

The right panel of the RSO's cockpit of the SR-71 contains the camera system controls, navigation system controls, radio controls, lighting and electrical system controls. (Tony Landis)

The RSO's instrument panel repeats some of the same instruments that are on the pilot's panel including the Triple Display Indicator (TDI), radio compass, fuel gauges and UHF distance indicator. The large Red remove before flight plate is covering the camera system view sight. This is the heart of the camera system and allows the RSO to see what is below the aircraft. Directly below the view sight is a radar display screen used in navigation. (Tony Landis)

This is the raised second cockpit of the SR-71B and SR-71C trainers. (Author)

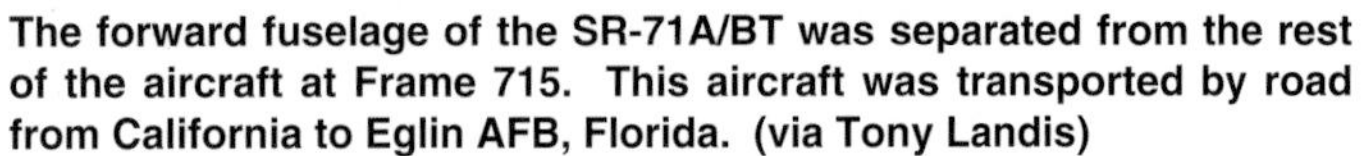

The forward fuselage of the SR-71A/BT was separated from the rest of the aircraft at Frame 715. This aircraft was transported by road from California to Eglin AFB, Florida. (via Tony Landis)

(Right) This is the Lockheed designed SR-1 ejection seat for the Blackbird. The double "D" ejection handle is Yellow with Black stripes. The headrest is Red, the seat was Black, while the back padding was in Medium Gray. (Tony Landis)

The chines are added to the round fuselage section as separate sections. Each chine rib section has numerous holes drilled in it to lessen the overall weight of the structure. This A-12 was the second aircraft built and it was donated to the USS INTREPID Museum in New York. (via Tony Landisß)

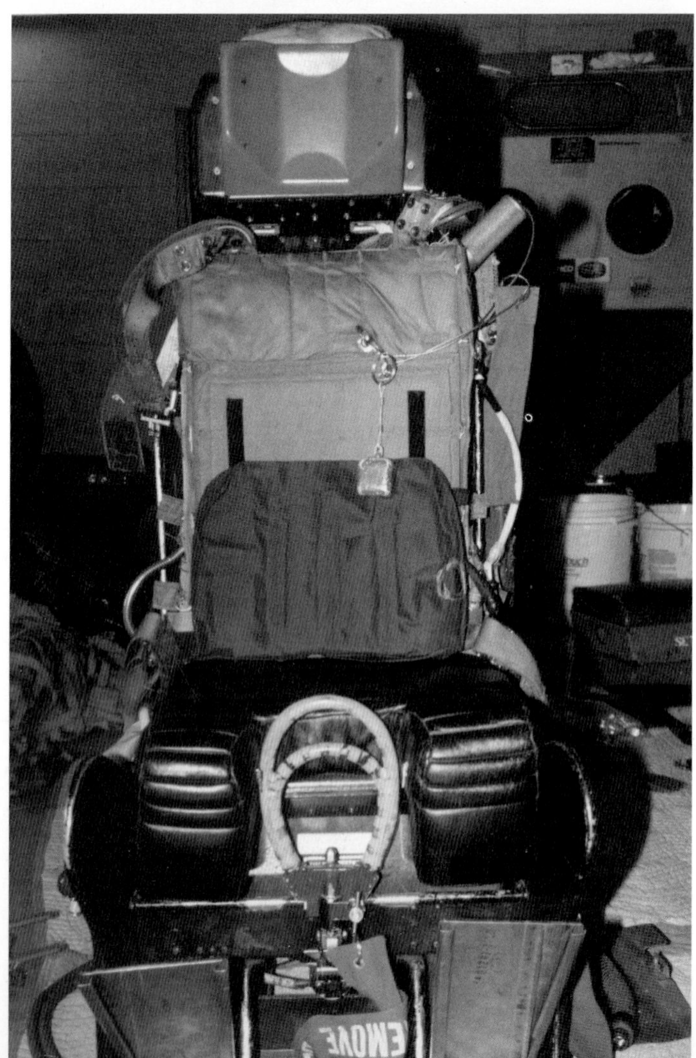